Lofted

Remarkable & far-flung adventures
for the modern golfer

Lofted

Remarkable & far-flung adventures
for the modern golfer

EDITED BY

William Watt
Dave Carswell
Jane Knight
Cameron Hassard

Hardie Grant

BOOKS

Foreword

→

*Locals from the Kabul
Golf Club in Afghanistan
gather for their regular
9-hole weekend round.*

*Photography by
Andrew Quilty*

People think we're a little crazy. Wandering around out there with a bag of sticks, chasing a little white ball around a paddock. In sunshine or rain. Jumping for joy, or slumping to defeat. Laughing or crying, and every emotion in between. Clamouring through the bushes or tall grass, searching and hoping to find a wayward strike. Getting up before dawn, on a weekend, for that prized first tee time. Dodging snakes, alligators, bugs, bears and even bombs. Leaning into the wind, sand blasting our faces as the dunes shift around us. Treading barefoot into the shallows to play a ball resting on the shoreline, with the faint hope of saving just a single shot. Sacrificing our backyards to hitting nets, and office floors to putting mats. Gizmos, apps, tips and gear. How deep do you want to go?

In the mind of a non-golfer, the question is inevitably 'why?' Why do we do it? What's the attraction of golf? And to explain it isn't so easy, because for a thousand golfers there are a thousand different answers. Golf is a game that caters for, and challenges, the mind of every player. The way we interact with golf reflects our very nature. So I can only answer the question from my perspective. But like a giant Venn diagram with a hundred interlocked circles, perhaps there's some overlap with your own love of the game.

For me, it's the feeling of endless discovery. The quest for new experiences and unseen horizons. Those moments of surprise and delight – mini-epiphanies that pop up at the most unexpected times. Because no two golf shots are ever the same. You could play the same course every day for a thousand years and still never hit the exact same shot twice. When you take this fundamental truth and then add in the endless variety of different courses, designed by different architects, played with different people, in different countries, in different conditions, then you have a recipe for a pursuit of unlimited possibilities.

Lofted is the culmination of four years of chasing these possibilities. Both literally – on the road playing courses around the world – and vicariously, through our amazing network of contributors, who are pursuing their own version of the game. Through the pages of *Caddie Magazine,* the founding team of Dave Carswell, Jane Knight, Cam Hassard and I have sought to spread the word of this great game through a lens unlike anything that has come before.

In this book, you'll read of golf adventures from truly remarkable destinations and the fascinating people we met along the way. From a war zone to a billionaire's playground. From vineyards in France, to a Malaysian rainforest, to a canyon at the foot of the Himalayas. Both the world's longest golf course and the world's longest golf hole. The old and the new. The rugged and the refined. If we found all this in four years, imagine what a lifetime in the game can bring?

We hope this book will inspire you to explore and see golf not just as the world's greatest game, but an opportunity to experience different environments, diverse cultures and meet wonderful people along the way.

Contents

The New and Old in Tasmania

TASMANIA
·   ·
AUSTRALIA

Spend some time around a golf course in Australia and you can count the seconds until you overhear 'Barnbougle' spoken about in hushed tones. We thought it would be a good place to start our adventure into the world of golf. And it was.

Words by Jack Carswell
Photography by William Watt & Dave Carswell

←

Players move up the 17th fairway at Barnbougle Dunes.

↙

The Great Forester River divides the two courses, Barnbougle Dunes and Lost Farm.

Jack Carswell worked at Barnbougle for nine years — first as a caddie and then as a greenkeeper.

I first walked Barnbougle Dunes a few years prior to its December 2004 opening, at a time when nearby Bridport was known only for its fishing and wild New Year's Eve parties. Tours of the course-to-be were offered to those interested, or as many people that could pile into the back of a LandCruiser. The notion of people travelling to sleepy Tasmania to play golf on a potato farm seemed pretty far-fetched, even to a golfing fanatic of twelve years. The tour ambled through the dunes on the front 9, driving each hole as it was to be played even though a preliminary routing was all that had been conceived. We stopped at a few locations to reference the map with the contours and proposed green locations. The point was made by the guide that very little earth moving would be required to maintain the true links feel, a promise that was certainly honoured. Years later, in a conversation course co-designer Mike Clayton attributed the difficult task of routing the course to the original topography created by the wind and sand, maintained over the years by the marram grass.

BARNBOUGLE DUNES

Barnbougle Dunes was the brainchild of Greg Ramsay, a golf tragic (he would say entrepreneur) who grew up on Australia's oldest golf course, Ratho Farm in southern Tasmania. Ramsay stumbled across the land, owned by potato and cattle farmer Richard Sattler, after having spent time in Scotland developing a deep passion for links golf. Bridport was a regular holiday destination for Ramsay and his family and it wasn't long before he found the highest point on the hill to gauge the depth of the dunes over at Barnbougle, within sight of Bridport town across Anderson Bay. Ramsay contacted Sattler by phone to discuss the idea of a golf course, however initial attempts were met with extreme hesitation. In fact Ramsay was labelled a madman. It wasn't until Ramsay arrived unannounced on Sattler's doorstep that he was taken seriously. After some serious persuasion and a few Scottish whiskies (I'm guessing), the links land was offered for the experiment, with Sattler having little to lose. He considered the land effectively useless – potatoes don't grow particularly well in sand and cattle prefer greener varieties of grass. Fast forward twelve months and Ramsay had Mike Keiser (owner of golfing mecca Bandon Dunes, Oregon), Tom Doak (renowned golf course architect) and Mike Clayton (former Australian professional turned course architect) in agreement that a world-class golf course could be built at Barnbougle.

And so it was: the birth of Barnbougle Dunes. Between the time the idea had been launched to the media and the opening, a lot had been said about the expectation of people travelling the world to play golf in Tasmania. I too had my doubts until the official open day when I caddied 36 holes and didn't meet one Australian golfer. Granted, there was never going to be an endless supply of cashed-up Americans, but it was clear that this golf course was something special and that the golfers would come from all corners of the world. And boy, did they ever! The numbers over the ensuing years have been phenomenal. As the course started to mature, the accolades began to roll in, with the course immediately ranked in the world's top 100, and soon becoming Australia's best public-access golf course.

Typically, with any great golf course there will be a number of holes that are spoken about with awe at the 19th and on golf trips for years to come. For Barnbougle Dunes it could be said that it is easier to speak of the less spectacular (yet still visually enticing) holes 1 and 2. Everyone who I caddied for would be blown away by the natural beauty and elegance of the first few holes without knowing what lay ahead of them. The stretch from the 3rd to the 7th provides some of the most mind-blowing visuals of any course in the world, from the behemoth bunker protecting the direct line to the 4th green, to the postage stamp green of the aptly named 7th, 'Tom's Little Devil'. Both holes play easy on paper, yet they've seen the demise of some of the best golfers in the world.

The course was designed with the prevailing north-westerly winds in mind – all the short holes play into the wind and the majority of the lengthy holes are downwind. The exception to the rule would be the 17th and 18th, both long par-4s stretching along the coast back into the wind, making holding onto a good round difficult. Many of the great golfing holes in the world tend to be drivable par-4s, of which Barnbougle Dunes has two (arguably more if you hit it like Bubba).

LOST FARM

It wasn't long after Barnbougle Dunes etched its name in must-play lists across the world that the concept of a second course was conceived. Anyone with a keen eye would have noticed the spectacular landscape across the Forester River, which runs adjacent to the 15th of the old course – a perfect setting for the Barnbougle story to continue. It would have been the easy option to keep Barnbougle course designers Doak and Clayton on board for this project. The area's remarkably dissimilar topography would have provided a strong contrast even if it had been crafted by the same architectural team. Yet Richard Sattler was determined to offer a completely unique experience to that of the older course. He enlisted the help of prolific course designers Bill Coore and Ben Crenshaw, whose handiwork is stamped all over courses like Friar's Head and Pinehurst No. 2.

With more dramatic topography and overall land area available to work with they were able to explore their absolute limits in course design. An experience completely removed from the original course, Lost Farm provides golfers with an opportunity to experience the transition from rugged coast to farmland. It's a style of course only possible on some of the most remote land in the world. There were so many great holes available that they ended up with 20 instead of 18. Two short par-3s were left in the mix and act as the perfect segues between the holes either side, with hole 20a perfectly positioned to square off any outstanding ledgers at the end of the round.

←
The par-3 6th at Lost Farm.

↗
Hole 13a at Lost Farm is a delightful par-3 nestled in the dunes.

→
The 6th green (right of frame) and 7th at Barnbougle Dunes (centre frame) known as 'Tom's Little Devil'.

Lost Farm is remarkably different to Barnbougle Dunes, a product of both the natural landscape and the vision of the designers. Working with more length perpendicular to the coast, course designers Coore and Crenshaw achieved a variety of hole orientations that work well with the prevailing coastal wind. This doesn't mean it hasn't had its fair share of coastal holes – in fact some argue that the holes hugging the water at Lost Farm are better placed to expose the views of the Bass Strait. Each hole leaves the shot placement and hole management squarely in the hands of the golfer, which is perhaps the biggest difference in course styles from the Dunes. Whereas the Dunes enforces a straightforward approach, Lost Farm grants the golfer more discrete options off the tee, as well as alternatives when approaching the green. That is encouraged by the vast area that many of the fairways cover, requiring twice the number of sprinkler heads to irrigate – good news for the erratic drivers out there. While there is certainly more forgiveness in fairway width, the portion between fairway and thick marram grass rough is almost non-existent, another contrast to its neighbour across the river.

As with the Dunes, it's a heated debate as to what the signature holes are at Lost Farm. The 4th would be a frontrunner, despite measuring in at just under 100 metres. Built on Sally's Point (named after Richard's wife, Sally, who penned this area to be a great location for a future house) it sits atop a thin peninsula, with Bass Strait claiming anything right and the Forester River protecting the left side of the green. As with the 7th across the other side of the river, club choice can range from a short iron with no wind to a firm 6-iron if it blows the way it should. After you've got through that test, you're met with the harrowing 5th hole – a mammoth par-4 that follows the river around to the right over a 10 metre sand dune that allows just a sneak peek of the green from the tee to emphasise the arduous journey to a par. For me, it's the 14th, a drivable par-4 down the hill to a slightly elevated two-tiered green with an open and vast backdrop of nothing but ocean, reminiscent of the vistas associated with Ballybunion in Ireland.

A GREENKEEPER'S PERSPECTIVE

While there are enough differences to distinctly separate the two courses, there are a number of similarities that you might expect from a stretch of land separated by only a river. Both use the same grass mix, consisting primarily of fescue grass with minor creeping varieties added in small quantities to provide a consistent smooth playing surface. The fescue grass enables the same playing surface from tee blocks to the cup, meaning the transition from tee to fairway to green is almost unnoticeable. The perimeter cut of the greens is only mowed once a week to promote this topography. Fairways are mowed in such a way that you won't find any Wimbledon-like shadows, rather maintaining a more traditional divide down the centre of the fairway. Greens are mowed at around 5 mm and run at 8 to 9 on the stimpmeter, which is comparatively slow to many courses. When the wind is blowing, many of the greens become unplayable at higher green speeds. This grass length also allows extreme contours to exhibit consistent turf cover, adding to the visual serenity that both courses provide. A significant advantage at Barnbougle is its proximity to a consistent supply of fresh water. Located either side of the Great Forester River estuary, the course has a limitless supply, effectively rendering it immune to drought.

Bunker management has evolved over the years. One of the apparent flaws in the design of Barnbougle Dunes was the orientation of some bunkers with respect to the prevailing wind. Strong wind gusts would see the sand blown out of many greenside bunkers, resulting in greens covered in sand and bunkers with consistently changing geometries and gullies forcing unplayable lies. Greens staff would consistently be reshaping bunkers to their original shape and volume despite the intentions of the course designers. In a conversation between the greens staff and Mike Clayton, he suggested we leave the bunkers alone, remarking 'let them move and evolve, you're wasting your time'. That's real links golf right there. The added advantage of this approach is not having to rake bunkers as part of the maintenance schedule, rather leaving the wind to clean up players' footsteps.

The two big questions I have been asked a number of times are: which of the two courses are better? And will there be a third? To answer the former, it's a tough one to call. For the more astute golfers, the hidden gems and permutations possible with each hole of Lost Farm will most likely take favour. There is no doubt that Barnbougle Dunes will remain the favourite for the everyday golfer, with its meandering natural beauty and in-your-face visuals, uncommon to any course in Australia. But really, does it matter what anyone thinks? They are right next to each other. Play both enough times until you have made your own mind up! As for a third course, Bill Coore is currently drawing up plans for a 9-hole short course over the dunes east of the 14th at Lost Farm. However with Coore's reputation for breaking convention (after all, Lost Farm is 20 holes), who knows what he might find out there in the dunes. One thing is for sure, I'll be heading back there to find out soon enough.

↖

The 14th at Lost Farm is a spectacular short par-4 with an ocean backdrop and strategic options.

←

Course furniture is on point.

Ratho Farm is a charming retreat in the Tasmanian countryside that speaks directly to a golfer's soul. It's a historic link to the origins of the game in Australia and a peaceful place to contemplate the future of the game.

Words & Photography by Dave Carswell

←

Owner Greg Ramsay (left), with Lamberta in tow, offers Jack Carswell some background on the course redevelopment.

↙

The signature 3rd hole with the Clyde River running past.

The Scots must have thought they had the luck of the Irish when their ships moored in the Derwent River of Old Hobart Town in the early 19th century. They'd just reached the end of the earth and, having escaped the challenges of the industrial revolution in Great Britain, had arrived in search of a fresh bounty in the colonial outpost. If the cramped and deprived conditions of the sailboat proved to be an enduring test of resilience, the fat of the land must have been a welcome sight for the new arrivals. The territory of Van Diemen's Land (Tasmania) was spruiked as a destination of new beginnings. Hobart had been settled for nearly two decades, and, with the promise of fertile land, young men reaped the benefits of an exchange program where property and labour were traded for capital and professional investment in the new colony.

Alexander Reid was one such young Scotsman who, having anticipated his older siblings' inheritance of the local family farm, decided to try his luck by boarding the Antipodean-bound boat. After six months of travel, Reid – along with his wife and two children – spent a short amount of time in Hobart, before being granted a land parcel north of the primary settlement at the foothills of the Central Tablelands. The Reids banded together with other Scots in the area, and the township of Bothwell was born, named in honour of the Scottish village outside of Glasgow. The Reids crowned their own patch of land Ratho, in a patriotic homage to their village of origin on the outskirts of Edinburgh.

Setting to work plying the land, the Reids were motivated by the offer of additional property for improvements made to their original allotment. The farm began to take shape as a part of the rich farming community emerging from the shadows of post-convict-era Australia. Buoyed on by lucrative prices for his merino wool, Reid was granted further parcels of land in 1828. Aside from the unique Australian fauna, the Scots must have felt right at home in the new colony, with a temperate climate not too dissimilar to home, fresh water supplies from neighbouring mountains, and rich farming lands for sheep and cattle.

Outside of the natural contours of the landscape, the Scots also brought with them other reminders of home, with accounts from Arthur Reid (grandson of Alex) detailing the family's introduction of golf to the area using their supply of old clubs and balls.

The Reids held on to Ratho for over a hundred years, passing it down through each generation. Then in November 1935 the farm was sold to another Scotsman, Alexander Stenhouse, a successful agricultural tradesman in Tasmania. He bought the property as a base for his fishing expeditions into the highland lake district, as well as to provide inheritance capital for his grandchildren. The farm today remains in the hands of the Stenhouses with Greg Ramsay, a descendant of Alexander whose parents Richard and Mary took over the lease of the farm in 1982.

Perhaps it was Greg's Scottish blood that spawned his interest in the game of golf and penchant for a dram of whisky. No doubt his time tinkering on the family property would have given him some inspiration. Having graduated from University of Tasmania, Ramsay went on to spend his early adulthood enriching his golfing experience with world travel, including a year-long stint at St Andrews. He returned to Australia at the age of 25, with the drive and creative nous to convince a Scottsdale potato farmer to build what would become one of the world's ultimate golfing experiences in Barnbougle Dunes.

Today his entrepreneurial fingers spread to many different pies, from destination golf consultancy to worldwide whisky distribution (and consumption). At the heart of his many and varied projects is the recent transformation of Ratho Farm into a contemporary golfing destination. The project pays homage to the history of the game in the Bothwell area, as well as shedding new light on the understanding of unique golfing experiences.

Starting with the original homestead and neighbouring buildings, the infrastructure of the farm has been transformed to create a luxurious yet homely accommodation experience teeming with character. The convict-built structures remain, with some original features including exposed walls and shortened doorframes, coupled with tasteful contemporary conveniences and comforts. Each suite is a fishing cast–length from the Clyde River, which ambles peacefully throughout the property providing guests with the lure of rainbow trout fishing.

The little snippets of history, interwoven into the modern stimulations, are understated aspects which service the overall experience. For example, former Melbourne Cup winner The Assyrian was brought to Ratho to stud the year after its victory in 1882. The tradition lives on, as Ramsay cheekily points out that the mounting room is now the honeymoon suite, with the cabin's deck providing the best view of the river.

While the farm's structures form the heart of the property, the surrounding golf course is the veins of the operation, pumping life into all four corners of Ratho. The track has recently undergone a substantial redevelopment to reclaim lost holes and provide modern additions to form a complete 18-hole championship course. The original 12 holes were inspired by the Prestwick Golf Course (an early Old Tom Morris design), with 6 holes heading north of the homestead and 6 holes heading south towards the township of Bothwell. The southern 6 holes were abandoned after the war, with subsequent changes to the neighbouring roads also disrupting the layout of the course.

Using historical photographs, scorecards and (no doubt whisky-soaked) anecdotes, Ramsay has been at the helm of the restoration of the lost 6 holes and the further development of 6 new holes, to create a course that is historically rich while still challenging contemporary expectations. The honesty box for green fees, historic outhouse (toilet) and square greens (which were traditionally used to form four-corner barriers to prevent sheep access) all bring an everyday and casual approach that cements the public-access course as a welcoming and fun destination for golfers of all persuasions.

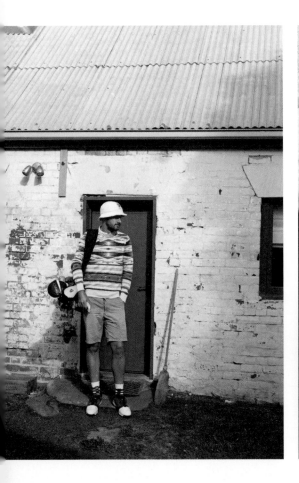

←
Convict-built cottages now provide quaint but comfortable accommodation on site.

←
Hickories are available for hire for those embracing the historic side of the experience.

→
Bothwell with a living, breathing history.

On paper, first-time players may question the apparent lack of length on the scorecard. Ratho is arguably far more challenging to those who hit it the farthest, a testament to both its original and restored routing. The hazards come in all shapes and forms, which is a welcome relief from the typical sand and water features of most other courses. Shot selection will often require a predetermination of which side of the stone fence or hedge will be ideal to attack the green from – without impediment from the veggie patch or shearing shed.

Ramsay admits to some challenges in balancing the expectations of players whilst ensuring the reputation of the course stands above the twee nature of its historic ties. The course had previously taken advantage of the neighbouring sheep farm to provide free lawn-mowing services to the fairways, but has recently restricted animal access to ensure the grass is in premium shape all year round. Even though the vast majority of fences protecting the square greens have been removed, many of the original timber sleepers and steel posts remain in place at each corner of the green as a reminder of the previous greenkeepers' inability to differentiate between fairway and putting surfaces. Mulligans are permitted, should your ball come into contact with the artefacts.

If you left your caddie at home, you are welcome to enlist the services of Lamberta, the domestic lamb responsible for guiding visitors on the course and providing (strangely patronising) bleating commentary on mis-hits and bad balls. Check ahead of time that she hasn't been sacrificed for carvery. And if the farm's highland cow isn't enough of a reminder about the communal links to the motherland, you can also head to the Nant distillery further upstream to enjoy another Scottish indulgence in local whisky production.

While it seems that multimillionaires and large investor groups are falling over themselves to find angular cliffs, virgin land and rockstar golf architects to design magazine listicle golf destinations for the Instagram crowd, the farm at Ratho proves that designing a desirable experience doesn't have to be remote or out of reach for the aspirational golfer. It may be easy to dismiss the Ratho golfing experience as novel, but the care and attention to detail of recent refurbishments serves to highlight a pivotal slice of Australian golf history and certain old-world charm that is hard to replicate.

There needs to be more experiences like Ratho that bridge the gap between community golf and destination travel. It's further proof that a memorable golf experience doesn't have to come with an equally memorable price tag. The history, honesty and integrity of this little Scottish oasis in the middle of Tasmania will be enjoyed by generations of golfers to come.

Caddie Tips:

· Holes 3 and 4 would stand out as two great holes on any golf course, particularly so in the Tasmanian Highlands. Hole 3 was lost to the construction of the adjoining road and bridge in the 1980s and has been restored with a split dogleg fairway with a Biarritz-style green, requiring three well-placed shots to have a chance at birdie. The 4th skirts the River Clyde and presents itself as a two-shot hole despite appearing on the card as a par-3. The challenge here is to choose a club from the tee without referring to the scorecard for distance. We would tell you how we fared but that would spoil the surprise.

· A stretch of the back 9 can be played in reverse, a concept originating at St Andrews and recently exploited at Forest Dunes Golf Club in Michigan with the Tom Doak–designed Loop. We suggest you discuss with Ramsay the idea and merits then decide for yourself which direction these holes play the best; the jury is still out.

· If you have ever fancied playing a round with Hickories, this is the place to do it. Don't be afraid to wager against well-equipped playing partners, since much of the trouble can be avoided with the reduced length that Hickories provide.

· Don't rely too much on advice from Lamberta; she has the wool pulled over her eyes.

Picturesque vistas through the farming communities in the Tasmanian Central Tablelands.

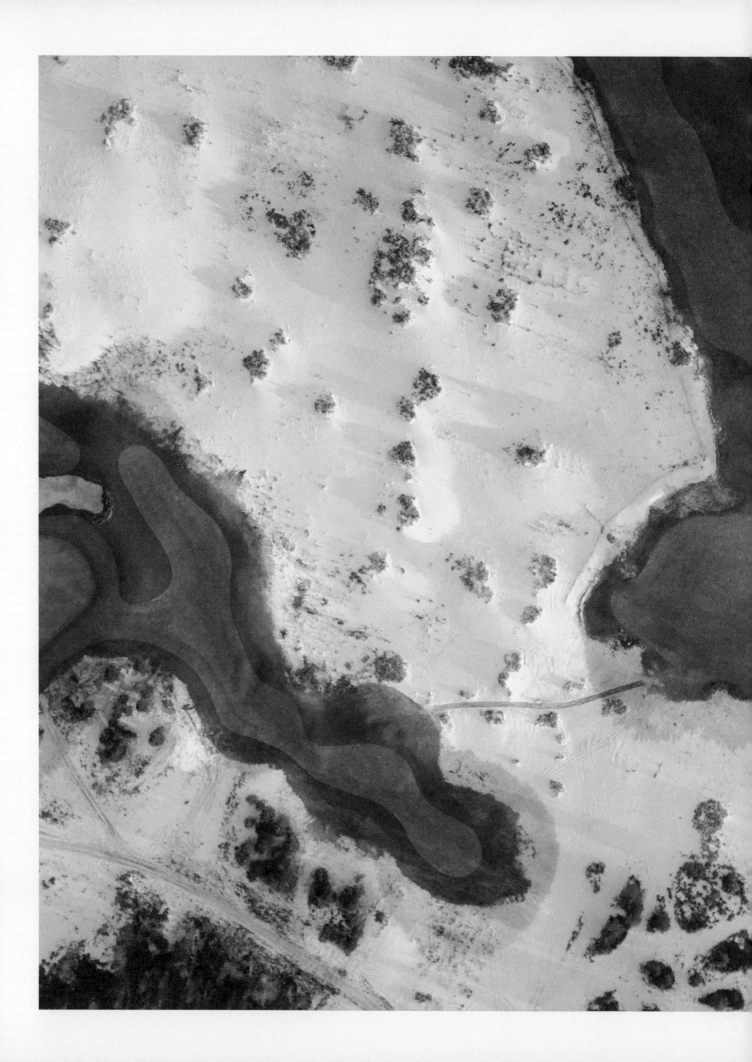

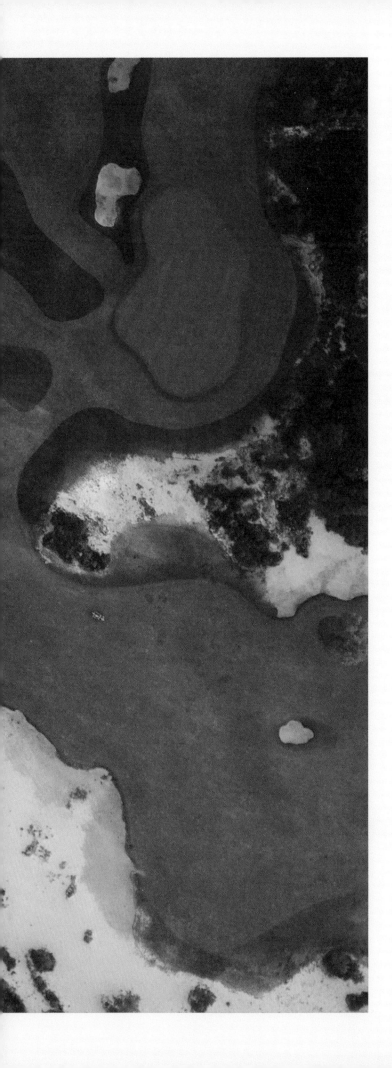

Sand Valley

WISCONSIN

•   •

U.S.A.

In search of an authentic American golf experience, Jack Carswell and William Watt travelled to Chicago and hit the road.

Words by Jack Carswell
Photography by William Watt

←

The unusual scale of the design is immediately obvious at the 1st green on Mammoth Dunes.

↙

Native plants and grasses in the sandy waste areas.

Our Sand Valley experience began as many others do – getting lost in the middle of Wisconsin. A short four hours north-west of Chicago, our satellite navigation system went into meltdown in its attempt to find the exact location of the newest golfing destination in the Midwest. In its defence, a review of Google Maps the next morning not only highlighted the remoteness of Sand Valley but begged the question: how was this land discovered for golf? Acres of nothing but red pine plantations free of any major body of water, a key ingredient in the majority of recent standout courses. It took a Chicago businessman trekking through the area with his wife in 2012 and a call to prolific golf course developer Mike Keiser (the man behind Bandon Dunes among others) before a location scout was sent to the sandy forest. Despite the lack of ocean, Mike must have liked what he heard. A vast landscape of glacial sand with enough acreage to give any architect free rein – complete with predetermined blowout bunkers (really, you should check out Google Earth).

We set up camp in 'The Clubhouse', a set of upscale modern suites adjacent to the main clubhouse overlooking the 1st tee of Mammoth Dunes, the David McLay Kidd–designed second course. DMK, who was responsible for the first course at Bandon Dunes, recently had his Castle Course at St Andrews rated a zero in rival architect Tom Doak's book *The Confidential Guide to Golf Courses (Volume I)*. The vista from our room over the 1st and 18th fairways of Mammoth Dunes hinted that the same wouldn't be said of this place.

Against all advice we decided to play Mammoth before Sand Valley. 9 holes were available for preview play (we visited before its official opening in 2018) and we had travelled too far to not whet the appetite. From the outset it was clear that DMK has left little sand without turf, with some of the fairways seemingly measuring equally in width as they do in length. Mammoth by name, mammoth by nature. The target areas available from the tees were in the most part disconcerting as we began to regret our decision to head out without caddies. Wide-open fairways give the average golfer a good chance of scoring well, while strategically placed bunkers and approach angles provide a tantalising test for the more astute player. Mammoth really felt like what Sand Valley was always going to be. Vast, natural-feeling fescue fairways rolling into deep expanses of sandy wasteland, lined by what remains of the pine plantations.

After an evening of night putting (the putting green has holes and mini-flags lit up by some form of magic) and cold drinks surrounding the fire pit, we caught the golfer's shuttle to the 1st tee of Sand Valley. A Coore and Crenshaw design, Sand Valley has been compared with Bandon Trails, another Keiser collaboration. It's hard to not be overcome with excitement looking out at holes 1, 10 and 18 from Craig's Porch, the halfway house we'll come back to later. One look at what lies ahead and it's apparent that whatever score is achieved, fun is guaranteed.

It all begins with a risk-reward short par-4. Almost drivable, it becomes a bogey hole, or worse, should a stiff, over-confident golfer take dead aim with – guess what – a sandy wasteland bunker waiting for anything left of the dogleg fairway. From here the challenges and opportunities come in droves. Each hole offers a birdie while threatening to question your decision not to throw a beach towel in the bag before heading out. For the golf architecture buffs, there are a number of template holes, including the 3rd, a Redan hole with a large ridge running along the right edge of the green. It's a good example of the playability offered to all, encouraging the low handicapper to execute a long iron over the bunker while allowing the average Joe to use the green shoulder to run one around the bunker to get to the green.

The enjoyment continues throughout the front 9 with a variety of shot-making required, despite the apparent breadth of landing areas. Many hazards are obscured from the tee: case in point presenting at the 6th with a slender bunker extending further into the fairway than can be seen from the tee, catching anyone without a caddie thinking they have struck the ideal line. The playability from the bunkers is refreshing and shouldn't be understated. Whereas many courses will penalise players to the nth degree for finding sand, Coore and Crenshaw have left the golfer options for their escape, depending on what they are willing to risk to save par.

One of our favourites was the short par-4 9th hole. Elevated tees with a drivable, elevated two-tiered green surrounded by deep pot bunkers and thick fescue, flanked by pine-riddled sand dunes, this hole really epitomises the best that golf and Sand Valley has to offer. The 9th is a hole you could play over and over again and still have no idea that it divides a lake – the only water on site, which supposedly has fish in it – and the halfway house, which serves some of the best tucker of any halfway house in golf. Ask

anyone who has played Sand Valley – the ice-cream sandwiches from Craig's Porch will get a mention. Numerous mouth-watering flavours are guaranteed to bolster your appreciation for mid-round grazing. Complementing the sweets are a selection of simple yet delectable tacos and sliders and at USD1.50 a piece, they have been forced to employ a marshal to remind players of their pace of play obligations.

After an unexpected feast it was a relief to find the inward 9 less hilly and more valley-like, with a number of punchbowl-style greens creating a few more scoring opportunities and less penal short game demands. The par-3s were again highlights, particularly the long 17th. With a huge punchbowl green invisible from the tee, the guesswork and anticipation walking from tee to green really captured the previous four hours of walking in a single hole, while emphasising the variety that we had come to appreciate. The last hole was a fitting finish to the day's play. A stunning uphill par-5 requiring two superb shots to reach the green with rolling fairways heavily guarded by sandy trouble. A huge multi-tiered green will likely see some matches decided by more putts than shots before ice-cream flavours are again hotly debated. Walking off the 18th at Sand Valley will have you wanting more.

If, like us, you breathe golf and enjoy its simple pleasures with a cold ale and bare feet, then Coore and Crenshaw have you covered with the 17-hole (yeah, they do things differently) par-3 course immediately adjacent to the Fairway Lodge, our recommendation for lodging if relaxed golfing is your style. The Sandbox course was originally slated as Quicksand, however this was quelled by Crenshaw supposedly because of its deathly connotations. Not yet open at the time of our visit, it looks like the perfect place to level any unsettled wagers left over from Sand Valley while squeezing in an extra bit of golf.

↓

Aerial of the Sand Valley course, another Coore and Crenshaw masterwork.

↓

Craig's Porch offers good value and perfect mid-round golf fare.

↑
*Jack kicking back
and watching groups
putt out on the 18th at
Sand Valley, ice-cream
sandwich in hand.*

An eye on Wisconsin: The (Unauthorised) Legacy of the Golf Courses of Lawsonia

Lawsonia, or Outlawsonia? Wisconsin's cherished yet little-known links paradise is an idyllic nook, but dig a little deeper into its traps and you might uncover a few gritty legends.

Words by Cameron Hassard
Photography by William Watt

Vagabonding through the American Midwest at the crest of this year's summer, intrepid Will Watt found himself on an unexpected pilgrimage deep in the Wisconsin woods. Days earlier at Michigan's Stoatin Brae Golf Club, he had encountered Riley Johns, an up-and-coming golf course architect and course shaper, who whispered the virtues of a little-known green paradise on the far side of the Great Lake. After swindling a match with Riley at the exclusive Shoreacres in northern Chicago – a round replete with putting green fairways and a caddie who was a dead ringer for Uncle Buck – Will defied interstate road trip conventions, balking the back end of a diabolically flatulent Mexican lunch to take Riley's advice as he hightailed, Al Capone style, over the border to the golf courses of Lawsonia.

Al Capone style? That's right, Al Capone style. When they weren't knocking back stiff rounds at Chicago's Green Mill or Kelly's Pleasure Palace back in the 1920s, Al Capone and the Chicago mob were often on the run, which usually meant one thing – Wisconsin. Just an hour's drive north of Chicago, the Wisconsin border gave the mob a convenient hideout when Chi-Town got too hot – and with it, a neat excuse for a few cordial rounds of golf.

HIGHWAY THROUGH THE DAIRYZONE

Well known as headquarters of the holy trifecta – beers, brats and cheese – one could easily add golf to the list for a Wisconsin superfecta. Adorned with glorious forests and farmland, America's Dairyland is also dotted with an array of world-class links. The four Pete Dye–designed courses at The American Club, the nearby Jack Nicklaus–inspired The Bull at Pinehurst Farms, and Erin Hills, host to the 2017 US Open, have all helped make the state one of the most sought after golfing destinations in America. What doesn't

hit the headlines so much are the stunning courses of Lawsonia, which remain one of America's most hidden gems with a less-than-conventional reputation.

One of the finest examples of Golden Era architecture in the US, architects Will Langford and Theodore Moreau designed Lawsonia during the Roaring Twenties after a sabbatical through Scotland, where they sketched and mapped the inspiration to create Lawsonia's multi-tiered greens, deep rough, and over ninety punishing pot-bunkers. Revered for his bold style, Langford had the elevated, undulating, wickedly fast greens and epic elevation changes constructed at Lawsonia using 1920s steam shovel technology, while the green at the boxcar hole 7 was apparently built around a train car filled with tar that had been shipped to the resort to build roads.

According to an unidentified source with knowledge of the area, the heritage links course, like many courses back in the 1920s, was supposedly frequented by the Chicago mob. While there's no hard proof that Al Capone ever slicked his spats over the Lawsonia mildew like he did the greens at Chicago's Burnham Woods, it's an assumption (and a required stretch for the sake of this article) that he might have.

'I'm not sure if Al Capone did in fact play,' says Lawsonia's PGA pro, Josh Carroll, 'but he was at the Green Lake Conference Center back in the day when it was "Millionaire's Paradise". One of the hotels at the conference centre used to be a casino, and a lot of old gangsters did in fact come up here.'

Great Lake is, after all, the relative halfway point between Chi-town and Capone's Northwoods hideout in Couderay, Wisconsin – the perfect nook for a road trip leg-rest and a swing of the iron in the heat of exile. Whatever the case, we can say a couple of things with certainty: the Chicago outfit of the 1920s and early 1930s couldn't get enough of Wisconsin, and in stubborn disregard for their lack of acumen, they cherished the game of golf.

MOB MULLIGANS: GOLF, CAPONE-STYLE

Well, a version of golf anyway.

Whether in Wisconsin or elsewhere, Capone and his crew golfed in the fashion that they conducted their business, as Luciano J. Iorizzo attests in *Al Capone: A Biography* – 'His [Capone's] rounds were devoted to having fun with his gangster friends who drank plenty each hole, gambled recklessly on the stroke of a ball and carried loaded weapons in their golf bags for use in emergencies.'

Al Capone golf, as Capone and his cronies knew it, carried a jovial and usually expensive set of rules. In a 1972 article for *Sports Illustrated*, Capone's caddie Tim Sullivan (then eight years old) recalled how his boss would run stakes at 500 dollars a hole – as well as the time he accidentally set off a .45 calibre revolver in his golf bag as he rummaged for a club, literally shooting himself in the foot.

Capone was capable of shooting most things, but he was unable to shoot for par. According to *Deadly Valentines* author Jeffrey Gusfield, Capone's love of the game couldn't change the fact that he remained for the duration of his life 'a terrible hacker and infamous destroyer of turf'.

Still, the golf bug persisted. If you ask Capone's niece Deirdre Marie Capone, who wrote a recent book on her infamous uncle, the mobster was a bona fide diehard, who allegedly escaped the US for a Scottish pilgrimage at the peak of his powers, just as the architects of Lawsonia, Langford and Moreau, had done.

'FAHGETTABOUTIT'

As with all empires large and small, the Chicago outfit didn't last. Capone was jailed well before the end of Prohibition, and while the family kept conducting business throughout the decades, the Golden Era was over. As for Lawsonia, after a few shifts of ownership during the post-war decades, the 1990s saw a dramatic overhaul of the property with the construction of a new woodlands course to accompany the heritage links course. To the operators' surprise, when digging up turf, Capone-era contraband was allegedly found buried in the ground near the main property: disused slot machines and sundry gangster paraphernalia (all fit for a sizeable evidence room at the 42nd Precinct). Bada-bing, bada-boom.

Nigh on a century since its inception, today there's little sign of lawlessness in and around the meticulous woods of Lawsonia – just natural splendour, and a nourishing day out. The original Scottish-style links course remains at the top of its game, while the modern Woodlands course offers a breezy afternoon session with its tree-lined fairways, local wildlife and unbridled beauty. All this, of course, is perfectly paired with a dose of the local catch at the Langford Pub's Friday night fish fry, or the Saturday night prime rib. If, however, you share the culinary mores of Will Watt, choose a few killer American pale ales with the best burger in the state – the aged cheddar supreme – a half-pound fresh beef explosion topped with seven-year-aged Wisconsin cheddar, applewood smoked bacon, sautéed mushrooms, and onions.

After a day at Lawsonia, it was an offer he couldn't refuse.

←
Dramatic land forms and minimalist style – an inland links of the highest quality.

Golf on Top of the World

POKHARA
·   ·
NEPAL

Jack Carswell leaves no green unturned by the buffalos, snow-fed rivers and incredible vistas of Nepal's Himalayan Golf Course.

Words by Jack Carswell
Photography by Dave Carswell & Sam Cooke

←

Local caddies take the lead on the 3rd fairway with the Himalayas in the distance.

↙

There are five river crossings throughout the routing, with snowmelt from the Himalayas providing a constant flow of pristine mountain water.

Amidst the foothills of the Annapurna ranges and nestled within the gorge of the Bijaypur River sits one of the most unique and awe-inspiring golf challenges in the world. The Himalayan Golf Course may be a relative newcomer to golf, but it has quickly cemented the title as one of the most unique courses found anywhere. Designed and constructed by ex-British Army Commissioned Officer Major Ram Bahadur Gurung and opened in 1998, the 18-hole layout features the extreme elevation changes one might expect of a golf course in a country hosting eight of the world's ten highest mountains.

Originally envisioning it as a 9-hole layout restricted by land, Major Ram gradually added hole by hole to fully encompass 18 holes, 13 of which sit 250 feet below the clubhouse in the river canyon. This has been facilitated by a number of shared fairways reminiscent of early Scottish architecture, including a repeat of holes 1 and 2 as 17 and 18 respectively. It's evident from the outset that minimal earth moving has taken place in this remote location, largely by necessity; but this proves true to the notion that nature provides a more enduring challenge than money can.

Holes 1 and 2 take advantage of the small parcel of land available between the clubhouse and mothballed resort construction that flank the entrance drive. While not overly inspiring, they provide a somewhat safeguarded introduction to Nepalese golf, with thick paspalum grass varieties and discrete well-placed hazards making a pair of pars to start with more than acceptable. The transition from the clifftop to the canyon is dramatically presented with the 3rd tee shot of the round: the drive shoots up into the Annapurna ranges before dropping for over ten seconds of hang time to a narrow fairway 200 feet below. Depth perception becomes critical as you plan your approach to the 3rd green, with anything over length falling victim to the snow-fed river. The front of this green, as with many here, is protected from the fairway maintenance herds by barbed wire fencing, reminiscent of the recently restored Ratho Farm in Tasmania, Australia's oldest operating golf course.

From here the course provides a sturdy test of the golfer's concentration and shot-making ability, as each hole is carved from the original landscape by thousands of years of erosion, creating varying elevations from tee to green, hole to hole. Making use of a naturally occurring island within the Bijaypur River, the course designer has created the signature 6th a 500 yard par-5 with two separate river crossings to reach the island green. If the 14th of St Andrews Old met with the 17th of TPC Sawgrass (the course in Ponte Vedra Beach, Florida, home to the annual PGA Players Championship), this would be the result. Believed to be the only island green in the world surrounded by a naturally flowing river, both the tee and green are separated to the west of the fairway by water, creating a tantalising opportunity to reach the island green in two shots for the brave or stupid. Two rows of pot bunkers located within the green complex line the approach area, encouraging the more conservative route of laying up to the right of the river to leave a short iron across the ice cold water, with two separate river crossings to reach the island green.

The majority of the back 9 meanders back and forth across the water, and every hole offers a quirk or two. Blind approaches over plateaus, clifftop greens, rickety bridges, locals picnicking, buffalo swimming in a greenside wetland – as with the rest of Nepal, there's always something to surprise. Our crew of local caddies, ball spotters and kids just enjoying the walk meant there were about a dozen of us navigating the course at times during the round, and everyone was feeling the heat in the valley as we neared the end of the loop (it was 34°C and not a lot of breeze to speak of on our visit). At about the 12th hole we realised we were low on water and golf balls (and a long, long way from the clubhouse), but our caddies quickly located a mountain stream with fresh water to fill our bottles with as well a backup supply of balls at a dollar each. (We churned through most of those as well and limped home with one ball each from our half-dozen starting allowance.)

The final challenge is traversing back up the cliff face to the par-3 16th. At only 160 yards one can be forgiven for taking an extra club to steer clear of leaving it short or right of the green from where a 200 foot plummet awaits. From the tee it's not immediately obvious where the green is located – the first to hit in our group launched one back down into the valley thinking the green was from where we had just come, to the amusement of the caddies and the bemusement of the rest of the group. (There was 'no fucking way' we were hiking back down into the valley having just ascended back to ground level.) In fact only the most hardy golfers will be keen to replay holes 1 and 2 for the 17th and 18th; after surviving the challenging 16th tee shot, the general feeling in our group was that handshakes were due and beer o'clock had arrived.

No great golf course is complete without a well-equipped 19th, for which the Himalayan golf experience satisfies. Set atop the cliff overlooking the course and mountain ranges, the clubhouse provides a spectacular backdrop to a well-earned Sherpa (Nepal's best beer as judged by us), which can be enjoyed most commonly with the chairman of the club, Bhuwan Gurung. If you feel as though you left a shot or two on the course, Bhuwan enjoys nothing more than the challenge of hitting the 6th green from the 3rd tee, only a stone's throw from the bar.

A course (literally) above all, the Himalayan golf experience is a timely reminder that golf in its purest and simplest form – without neatly manicured or tightly cut fairways and greens – can provide both a challenging and enjoyable test of skill and determination uncommon in the modern golfing world.

Wise Caddie Counsel

· Spring and autumn are the best times to experience Himalayan golf. With a subtropical climate, good visibility and uninterrupted views of the Annapurna ranges, Pokhara is already a popular choice for tourists. At these times you will also likely avoid a flooded 6th green, which can occur at the height of summer due to the melting snow upstream.

· The course is navigable by caddie only, as the transition from tee to fairway to green is almost indistinguishable as a result of the local sheep and goat herds administering the fairways. The caddies are sourced from the local area and can provide a unique insight into the Nepalese culture, while endeavouring to prevent the tumultuous climb back to the clubhouse for extra golf balls during your round.

· The greens run surprisingly true thanks to the hard work of ten full-time greenkeepers. While speeds vary naturally they offer a fair chance of making good scores when you have kept your ball on the straight and narrow.

↗
The bulk of the holes (13) sit within this canyon, crisscrossing the river and providing plenty of surprises.

→
Sam tees off on the long par-4 5th.

Himalayan Wonderland: The Road Diaries

'The most amazing golf course on earth' is a big call. It was a promise worth chasing to the foot of the Himalayas and pursuing on the back of a fleet of Royal Enfields.

Words by Daniel Vigilante
Photography by Dave Carswell & Sam Cooke

Dangerman Daniel Vigilante on surviving death, rebel life and missed connections on the great Himalayan road.

My trip to Nepal started like it ended – with airport dramas. A missed flight connection forced me to spend the night in Guangzhou, China, until the next flight to Kathmandu, a full day later. The annoyance, however, came with a silver lining: I got put up in a five-star hotel of my choice, an upper-middle-class micro-holiday, which I (as someone who bought the cheapest flight they could find) probably didn't deserve. So I wasn't complaining. Much.

Landing in Kathmandu later than planned meant my two days in the capital became little more than another layover. More logistical dramas reduced it further – the taxi couldn't find my hostel so I lost another two hours in a bicycle rickshaw searching for it. The next day we flew to Pokhara in a plane not much bigger than a kid's toy model. The twenty-minute flight provided a breathtaking view of the Himalayas, which were at eye level and kept me distracted from the terrifying ordeal that any rational person would otherwise feel in a toy plane.

Pokhara is the second largest city in Nepal, but to most tourists who stay in and don't leave the tourist district of Lakeside, it feels like a charming little town. It's situated in a valley beside Phewa Lake, and the mountains rise very quickly – within 30 kilometres the elevation rises from 1000 to 7500 metres. The most striking peak you can see from Pokhara is Machhapuchhre, or 'Fishtail' mountain, and it photobombs every picture taken from the street. Pokhara is a mountaineering hub (it's the base for the famous Annapurna Circuit trek) and a beacon to the outdoorsy traveller. Here you can hike, raft, bungee, paraglide, play golf at one of the most scenic courses in Asia, and, of course, ride motorbikes.

Our crew – six Aussie wannabe rebels from a variety of walks of life, living in six different cities across three different countries – met up here to ride motorbikes and play golf. The motorbiking aspect was courtesy of Hearts and Tears Motorcycle Club, a business based in Pokhara that runs group motorbike tours primarily on Royal Enfield Bullets, the world's longest-living and arguably most handsome motorcycles. Originally British made and owned, and brought to India during Crown rule, the bikes have been wholly Indian made and owned since 1949, and still look incredible.

Hearts and Tears is owned and run by Matt, a friend I met as a fellow exchange student in Mexico City a decade ago. Hearts and Tears has grown to become one of the finest motorcycle tour companies in Asia, with spectacular tours on offer for beginners right up to biking aficionados. Three of us in the group were definitely in the novice skill range, having barely any motorcycling experience (one got up early and had a two-hour lesson on the morning that we were leaving). The fact that all bikes were manual only added to the challenge.

We started out from Pokhara on day one and headed to Bandipur, about 80 kilometres south. The newbies were fairly cautious on their big new toys and there was some wobbly handling and a number of stalled starts. But riding a motorised bike is a bit like riding a bicycle – once you've got it, you've got it. The learning curve was steep and it wasn't long before we were outmuscling the locals on scooters and asserting our place in the road hierarchy. Steppenwolf's *Born To Be Wild* became the soundtrack to the afternoon – at least in my head anyway.

We made it to Bandipur by late afternoon: a quaint hilltop town along a mountain saddle just 200 metre long and barely wide enough to accommodate a strip of buildings on either side of the main street. The last 8 kilometres of the road to Bandipur ascends 1000 metres, making it a challenging, winding incline where, I regret to admit, I stalled in full view of the crew, began to roll backwards, and lost all the riding credit I thought I was building.

Our accommodation in Bandipur was a beautifully restored old-style inn with dark wooden detailing, smoky old bricks and low ceilings. It felt a bit Dickensian, except it had wifi. We enjoyed a few well-earned beers and reminisced on the day's ride, patting ourselves on the back for surviving. We were served a feast of house-roasted pork, potato and gravy and retired by 9 pm due to sheer exhaustion. The pre-dawn ride the next morning rewarded us with one of the best sunrises you're ever likely to see, gaining a brilliant vantage point overlooking the Dhaulagiri and Annapurna mountain ranges. It put everyone in a good mood for the ride ahead.

Day two saw us head for Chitwan National Park, Nepal's oldest national park and, as the brochures will tell you, home to the Bengal tiger. The ride itself was one of the most gruelling as there was a long stretch of extremely bumpy and dusty gravel road populated by big ugly trucks, roadworks and boulders. It was a hellish section but it made the cold beer upon arrival at our safari accommodation all the more satisfying. The guided forest walk we took through the Tikauli Jungle didn't show any tigers but we did see a few rhinos, which justified the price of the ticket. Our accommodation boasted wild elephants roaming free behind the property. The food in the evening, as always, was fit for a motorcycle gang.

Day three was the longest ride: 160 kilometres to a town called Tansen. After another ultra-scenic lunch stop, the late afternoon ride was one of the best: a lively exploration through a labyrinth of small alleyways, with the loud roar of the bikes attracting everyone's

attention. Sunset fell for the final 10 kilometres along a ridgetop, a stretch memorable for its colour and pastoral serenity. We spent the evening at an organic farm nestled in a quaint valley and were served the world's tastiest smoked bacon, among other things, before retiring beside a hearty fire. The morning revealed the real charms of this rustic farmhouse and, after a smashing breakfast with the leftover bacon, we were all a little sad to leave knowing it would be our last day looking tough on a bike.

The ride from Tansen back to Pokhara was probably the most fun, as by this stage we were all utter pros on the bike (if I do say so). The winding road through the luscious 'dragon's tail' hillside was almost desolate, perfect for the mad-dog bikers we had become. When we finally came roaring back into Lakeside, Pokhara, the beaming smiles on all of our faces were hard to shake.

The relief at not dying was palpable and manifested itself in a drinking binge by the lake, where we talked through and embellished the highlights. The next few days in Pokhara were spent recovering, reflecting, playing golf, and buying pashminas and handwoven rugs. One last overnight hike to the aptly named Australia Camp brought another surreal sunrise, and I began to convince myself that perhaps I could become a morning person. The gang disbanded over the next twenty-four hours, and after some more airport dramas, which nearly broke my spirit, I finally made it home. My heavily pregnant wife gave birth a few weeks later, and we all lived to tell the tale. Just don't tell her I came off the bike twice.

←

Traversing rough terrain aboard our classic Royal Enfields.

↗

Local children on their way to school above the clouds.

→

The mountainous terrain throughout Nepal makes for an epic ride experience.

The Home of Golf

ST ANDREWS · · SCOTLAND

Serious golfers often quote that a visit to the place golf calls home is a must do at least once in their lifetime. St Andrews was host to the 2015 Open Championship, giving us reason to make the pilgrimage to soak up the history and discover the origins of the game.

Photography by William Watt

←
Previous pages

(Left) The Old Course prepares for the Open.

(Top right) The Royal and Ancient Golf Club of St Andrews clubhouse.

(Bottom right) The bunkering on the Old Course is no joke.

↖

Zen-like bunker work during the Open Championship.

←

A traditional marching band performs at the Open marching up the 1st fairway.

↑

Distinctive sod bunkers on the 17th with the beautiful old town of St Andrews beyond.

↖
Humps and bumps at the Castle Course.

←
The Castle Course is ten minutes east of St Andrews and is a somewhat controversial addition to the golf offerings in the area.

↑
Crowds from the Open Championship line the streets of St Andrews.

The Templates

Words & Illustrations by Mike Cocking

The golfing bug took a firm hold of Charles Blair Macdonald at the home of golf – St Andrews. The Chicagoan had moved there as a teenager to complete his matriculation – what we would know today as the last year of high school. During his time there he learned the game from none other than Old Tom Morris and his son Tommy. Two pretty handy mentors to introduce a newcomer to the game!

On his return to the US he helped promote the game through his involvement and design of the first 18-hole course in the country – Chicago Golf Club. The success of this project led Macdonald to change careers from stockbroking to golf course architect – a term he made up – and as the game became more popular so too did his new calling. By 1908 an opportunity arose to create a new course in the beautiful sandy terrain alongside Peconic Bay in Southampton, New York. This would become his seminal design, the National Golf Links of America.

To create America's first great golf course Macdonald decided he must travel back to the British Isles and study the great holes. On his travels he would identify around twenty templates, which stood apart due to their strategic interest. He then carefully arranged the best combination of eighteen onto the South Hampton site.

The names may be familiar, as are the courses where he drew inspiration from. Other than the Cape, which is credited to Macdonald as an original idea, the templates included: Road (17th on the Old Course), Cardinal (3rd at Prestwick), Dell (5th at Lahinch), Redan (15th at North Berwick), Alps (17th at Prestwick), Double Plateau (origin unknown), Biarritz (3rd at Biarritz in France), Eden (11th at the Old Course), Short (4th at Royal West Norfolk), Long, Sahara (3rd at Royal St Georges), Bottle (12th at the Old course at Sunningdale), Leven (16th at Lundin Links), Perfection, Punchbowl, Gibraltar and Postage Stamp (8th at Troon).

He had a trusted partner to assist at the National by the name of Seth Raynor, a non-golfing surveyor who would later be heavily influenced by Macdonald and the templates at the National when he embarked on his own career as a designer. So too would Charles Banks, a lesser-known but highly skilled teacher-turned-architect from Yale University who joined Raynor full-time after assisting in the construction of their wonderful course. Together they were some of the greatest designers of the Golden Age and produced many fine golf courses including Chicago, Yale, NGLA, Shoreacres, Fishers Island, Yeamans Hall, Mid Ocean, the Creek Club and Sleepy Hollow.

Whilst Macdonald, Raynor and Banks championed the use of the templates, they were by no means unique to these three prolific architects. Other Golden Age architects would occasionally use templates as inspiration, including George C Thomas with his long Redan 4th at Los Angeles Country Club, Alister MacKenzie (who talked of building an Eden hole at Royal Melbourne West) and AW Tillinghast, with his Redans at both Philadelphia Cricket Club and Somerset Hills.

After the Golden Age, templates fell out of favour and were perhaps underappreciated, with many altered and few new examples built. However, in recent times, as part of the game's second Golden Age, there are now many new versions being built, with the Redan and Biarritz greens being especially popular. Debate rages over whether the templates were highly creative or just plain unoriginal and formulaic. As architects we regularly draw inspiration from great examples of design and not a day goes by where we don't compare the ground in front of us to something vaguely familiar at a highly rated design. However, it is how each hole is adapted to the landscape that remains the most important aspect of the design process.

Alps

The original Alps is at Prestwick. Old Tom left St Andrews for the West Coast after a dispute with his then-boss Allan Robertson and laid out this wonderful links for the new club. He stayed on as curator and competed in the first open played there in 1851 on the 12-hole course.

The Alps is one of its quirkier holes. A medium to long par-4 involving a straight-away tee shot laid up short of a high dune. The punchbowl-style green sits blind on the other side of the hill with a large Sahara-style bunker guarding the front.

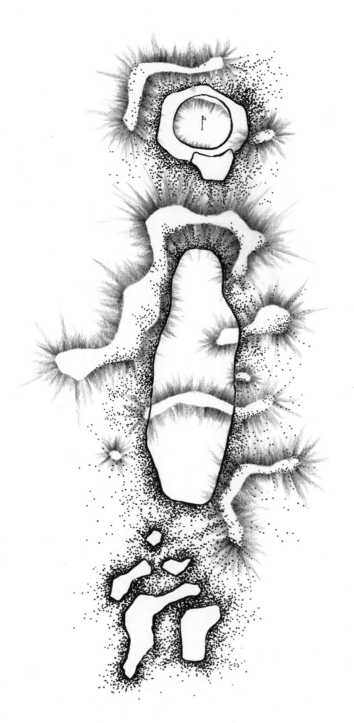

Biarritz

The original has its name derived from Willie Dunn's Biarritz Golf Club in France (the par-3 3rd hole) but surely Dunn or Macdonald also drew inspiration from the fabulous 16th green at North Berwick.

Biarritz holes are typically long par-3s with a very large green split into two fairly equal sections – front and back – using a deep swale that runs the full width of the green to divide the two plateaus. Sometimes the front plateau is maintained as fairway rather than green with only the back section available for putting but I think the best examples have the option of a pin at the front too. In modern times the Biarritz-style green has been adapted to par-4s and par-5s with some including the option of a swale large enough for a pin position.

Biarritz greens work well in encouraging a running shot, which in the current era of driver-pitch play, is to be championed. Any time the pin is at the back, the best play is a low shot that lands somewhere near the front and runs through the swale. The option to fly a ball all the way to the back section is far less appealing as balls that land in the swale typically stay there and landing over the green is bogey territory.

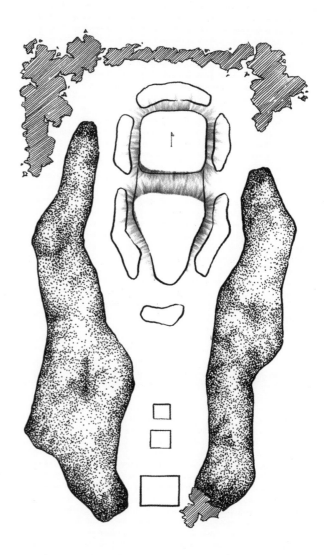

The Cape

Unlike the other well-known templates, Macdonald's Cape hole was an original. His most famous version is in Bermuda, at the Mid Ocean Club, but his first came at the National Golf Links.

One of the most dramatic templates, the traditional Cape plays diagonally across water so the golfer has to decide how much risk to take on in order to have a shorter approach. The green is usually guarded at the back and sides with bunkers, water or, in the case of Shoreacres, a creek.

Redan

Macdonald described the Redan simply: 'Take a narrow tableland, tilt it a little from right to left, dig a deep bunker on the front side, approach it diagonally and you have a Redan.'

But he failed to mention one really important point. Key to the concept is a green that falls away from the player on the tee, with a high point on the right (lower on the left) that shoulders a running ball in towards the middle of the green.

One of the most difficult elements to get right as an architect is a fall-away green and with modern green speeds, some old Redans have become borderline unplayable. Remember Goosen's US Open triumph at Shinnecock Hills?

Typically Redans require a mid-iron and the prudent play is to land short and run it up the slope rather than land on the green where the ground slopes away. The best miss is long, where the player has a relatively easy putt or chip back up the slope.

I was surprised when I first saw the original and just how blind it was from the tee with the short hill and bunkers blocking much of the view.

A nice variation is where the putting green runs over the front of the green and down into the valley below, making a running shot even more enticing. The fantastic par-3 7th at Chicago is such an example.

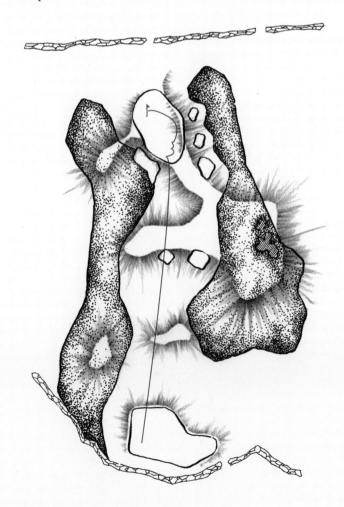

Road

The Road is one of golf's most famous: the 17th on the Old Course with its blind drive over the old railway sheds, the road and the wall behind the green. But these aren't the reasons the Road hole is such an incredible design.

The Road hole is all about angles. The fairway sits at a 45 degree angle from the tee much like a reverse cape tee shot. The narrow tabletop green then sits in the opposite direction, right to left, again at roughly 45 degrees. The amazing contours at the front of the green shoulder anything but the perfect approach toward the cavernous bunker, where Tommy Nakajima took 5 to escape in the 1978 Open Championship.

Originally the Road hole was a par-5 but nowadays plays as a long par-4. Other template versions also vary the par. At Macdonald's National it is a 5; at Chicago and Shoreacres it's a long 4. But the numbers matter little. Providing the hole is long enough to leave a long iron (or hybrid), the golfer has to land their ball short of the green and deal with the devilish contours and *that* bunker. ⚑

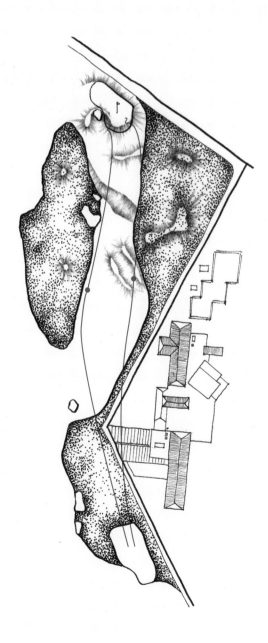

Silvies Valley Ranch

OREGON

·   ·

U.S.A·

Traversing fuel panic, ranch links and beaver fever in Grant County, Oregon.

Words & Photography by William Watt

←

The reversible layout at Silvies is aided by a zigzag design.

Generally speaking, one week is not typically enough time to plan a trip across the planet. But hey, things were pretty quiet at the office and how often do you get invited to a launch event that involved goat caddies? So here I find myself at the Vancouver airport, having missed my ambitious connection to Portland, cashing in a USD10 meal voucher at Starbucks and contemplating the last leg of a thirty-eight-hour journey from door to door.

The sunset flight down the west coast to Portland is ridiculously scenic – an unexpected bonus of the missed flight. Out the window of our turbo-prop are extravagant seaside communities, dense forests and hazy mountain peaks. Then, the distinctive shape of Mt St Helens comes into view, which I recognise immediately from a well-loved *National Geographic* issue covering its famous eruption in 1980 that caused the largest known debris avalanche in recorded history (and one that caused the mountain itself to lose 400 metres in height). Fifty-seven people were killed, primarily by the vicious pyroclastic flow that was released after the north side of the mountain collapsed. The resultant lahars (volcanic mudflows) completely destroyed over 600 square kilometres of pristine wilderness. In the weeks following, US President Jimmy Carter surveyed the damage and said, 'Someone said this area looked like a moonscape. But the moon looks like a golf course compared to what's up there.' Which reminds me why I'm here.

Picking up my hire car shortly before dark, it's a race to get out of the city and put a dent in the 303 mile drive eastwards before darkness falls. I make pretty good time, and twilight through the pine trees at the base of Mt Hood is spectacular. Before long it's just the road – whatever the high beams can illuminate – and a flickering GPS signal to my phone's navigation. About this time I notice the handy 'miles remaining' stat on my dashboard. In my enthusiasm to get some miles behind me I have thrashed the engine to the point where fuel is now an issue. The buffer between my destination and reserves is about sixty miles and dropping fast. I start coasting down hills and taking it easy going up them – techniques my thrifty grandfather taught me on road trips through rural New Zealand. But it isn't working. A wrong turn courtesy of the blue dot being MIA for about ten minutes doesn't help. I need fuel. It's now 9 pm and all the most populated places on the route have passed. I drift through tiny towns along the Ochoco Highway with nothing names like Mitchell and Dayville, no fuel in sight. Mt Vernon is my beacon in the night. I pull up at a station just as the sole employee is getting on her bike. I plead my case and she says 'I wish I could help y'all' in a voice so friendly that 'well, you can – please turn on the pump, I've been travelling for thirty-six hours and it would be a massive help' doesn't make it to my lips. With 20 miles remaining in the tank I pull into an abandoned Chevron and hope like hell one of my cards works. On the fourth (and last) attempt, it takes. Fuel flows into the tank like adrenaline into my veins. Which is handy because that's the only fuel I'm running on at this point.

Another hour on the road and I see the glorious SILVIES RANCH sign glowing in my headlights. Damon, the head chef, lives on site, and interrupts some downtime to show me to my room. Suddenly, I'm in luxury. Plush carpets, log cabin–style walls, a giant super-king bed with Pendleton wool blankets, a comfortable couch and a cold beer in the fridge. After nearly two full days on the move, I collapse into the comfiest bed of my life.

Up at dawn for a photography session, I find that I've landed on the set of a Western movie, except that nothing here is artificial. Pine trees, log cabins, meandering creeks surrounded by lush meadows, and hills covered in semi-arid scrub that stretch for miles in every direction. A minty, herbal smell of sage permeates the air, which is cool and crisp in the pre-dawn light. As the first rays of sun touch the lush fairways, I know I'm somewhere special.

Photographing a golf course before you've played it can be a bewildering experience – you have no idea what's what. But in this case it's doubly confusing, because Silvies' premiere course is a reversible routing. Based on the day's date, on odd-numbered days you play it clockwise (known as the Hankins course), and on even days counter-clockwise (Craddock course). It also has 27 green complexes, meaning that 9 of the greens are common to both courses, 9 are unique to Hankins and 9 are unique to Craddock. This gives the routing a degree of flexibility that allowed designer Dan Hixson to fully explore the landscape available at Silvies, whilst still bringing the host of advantages that a reversible course can bring. To quote Hixson: 'The reversible design supports sustainability in golf, which is of course very important to the philosophy and mission at Silvies Valley Ranch. It creates two unique layouts within the same footprint of land, utilising less resources.'

Having 27 greens also means that, unlike Tom Doak's Loop in Michigan, or indeed the Old Course at St Andrews, it's not as if you are approaching greens from the complete opposite direction each time. Indeed, many of the fully reversible holes here are situated in a zigzag formation, meaning you approach common greens from the same side, but at perhaps a 40 degree to 50 degree different angle from the previous day.

All this adds to a sense of adventure as I play the course for the first time. There is a lot of head turning on fairways and frequent references to the excellent course guide (also reversible) to try and figure out not only which hole I'm playing, but which hole I will be playing tomorrow. Whilst wayfinding on the course could be improved, as I complete a round on the Hankins I have a firm grasp of the entire layout, including a good look at what I'll be facing tomorrow on Craddock.

Exploring the land out here through golf is a joy – the serenity is unmatched. Even a gentle gust of wind can first be heard in the pines nearby, then the usually unheard sound of air moving against earth, washing over me with the scent of sage. During one photography session, I spot a deer far in the distance and send my drone over to capture it wandering down a fairway. It gets spooked and gallops to the undergrowth. A full eight to ten seconds later, I'm the one who is spooked, as I hear another deer approaching me from behind. I leap back into my golf cart and look around for the attacker. My heart is pounding. Nothing. Huh. I dismiss it initially and get back to work, but then think – I definitely heard footsteps approaching. Eventually I realise that it had to be the sound of that far-off deer galloping away, delayed by a slightly slower speed-of-sound at this altitude, and carrying so incredibly clearly that I perceived it to be a different animal moving within a few metres of me. It is a completely surreal experience.

In this environment, a well-struck drive echoes through the valleys, and the soaring ball flight, given an altitude of nearly 5000 feet, is really, really satisfying. Hixson has recognised this and offered at least a half-dozen elevated tee shots across the property. Some of which, like the 8th and 14th on Hankins, seem to offer an endless hang time, before your ball gently plops on the fairway 200 feet below (which, again, you can hear). The birdsong is frequent and beautiful, and standing on fairways surrounded by pine-covered hills brings a level of relaxation I wouldn't have thought possible given my relatively compressed time here.

Both courses are tremendously fun to play. There are options off every tee, a great variety of holes and every club in the bag is required. The bunkering across the course is a little too gentle for my tastes – as you'll read in our Sandbelt feature, bunkering in my hometown is a kind of a big deal. I would have loved to have seen some more aggressive shaping and bold faces around the course, especially given the terrain. But punishing the golfer is not the focus here; it's about fun, playability and relaxation, while still challenging the better players and posing strategic questions off every tee. The cleverly crafted run-off areas around the green complexes offer a variety of chipping and recovery shots – Texas Wedge players will be right at home here in Oregon – and provide the strongest defence to wayward approaches. Most holes have a bailout zone and a no-go zone, which asks players to take a risk if they want a good look at birdie. The steeply undulating greens are a heap of fun to putt on – creative players will enjoy taking the long road occasionally, where putting at right angles to the hole at the right pace makes for a pleasing journey. The pace on the greens is spot on, rolling out just enough to temper my aggression slightly, but with enough forgiveness to make the come-backers fairly straightforward.

There's a good flow to both directions of the routing. A broad, sweeping opening with views across the course, a middle 9 holes that bring a more secluded and intimate vibe as they meander up into the valleys of the nearby ranges, and then on the 14th of both directions, you bust back out into the expanses of the prairie lands for the run home. Not that there's any rush to complete your round – it's such a serene environment to be in that it's impossible not to relax. During our round one of our foursome, charismatic local sports radio presenter Michael Williams, is determined to get back to watch the World Cup semi-final. 'I'm just playing 9' on the first tee turned into 'maybe I'll just watch the second half' to 'okay one more hole' to 'I'll just watch the replay'.

I don't think Michael ever ended up seeing the match. Later that afternoon, we're out on a shooting range, rifles in hand, exploring the expanses of the ranch in awesome little 4WD buggies. We spot a massive herd of antelope (our guide reckons more than seventy head), a baby elk and its mother, the famous crabapple tree (where the local signature Horseshoe Nail cocktail gets its homegrown garnish), and even an early adopter beaver. Our guides are educated and passionate about the land, the animals and the guest experience. There's also a concerted effort to respect and communicate the history of the land the ranch now occupies, and to restore some of the riverways and meadows that were devastated by the removal of beavers in the early 1800s (removal is too kind a word here). At that time, Oregon was under a joint occupation agreement between Britain and the United States. The British were occupying the area primarily through the operations of The Hudson Bay Company: a global fur goliath, already with hundreds of years of trade under its belt since its founding in 1670.

A good example of how the reversible holes work, with the two greens at the top of frame being approachable from two directions.

→

The short course McVeigh's Gauntlet features optional goat caddies. Yes, you read that right.

As US interest in Oregon gradually increased, and the riches of fur became apparent, the HBC, under instruction from British hierarchy, went about creating a fur desert, thereby devaluing the land and making it less attractive to US pioneers. Whilst not constrained to Oregon, these missions, ominously named Snake Country Expeditions, wiped out hundreds of thousands of beavers in the space of just eight to ten years. As well as being incredibly brutal to beavers (and probably providing very cheap fur hats to Europeans) the policy proved to be an environmental disaster.

Why is all this important? You see, beavers are bloody hard workers. They spend their lives building dams out of sticks and branches collected from hardwood trees that grow along the banks of the river (which also happen to be their primary food source). These beaver dams have the handy side effect of slowing down the flow of a river, and, over time, can turn otherwise arid land into a huge sponge, capable of soaking up snowmelts throughout the summer and providing an abundant habitat for a variety of flora and fauna.

With the beavers gone, their dams fell into ruin and eventually washed away. The rivers began to streamline. The water ran right on through previously lush meadows and started to dig canyons as it went, which only further accelerated its progress. Trees that previously thrived in the moist ground near the river suddenly found themselves in an arid setting and quickly died. The few beavers that remained gradually lost their food source and construction materials. The arid-loving sage bush, previously confined to higher ground, began marching into the prairie lands. Before long the land was unrecognisable from before.

Silvies owners Scott and Sandy Campbell are now 'bringing back the beaver' to their property through targeted river projects that aim to reverse this entire process, step by step. First they have to slow the water down again to create the sponge effect – without that the willow trees won't grow and a beaver population will struggle to survive. They're doing this through the construction of artificial dams along the route of the river, encouraging a snaking route through the valley and creating rejuvenated meadows. The first of these projects, on a river that runs alongside the McVeigh's Gauntlet course, has been a raging success. The beavers are back in small but increasing numbers, the meadow is lush, and the sage bush is in retreat for the first time in centuries. Silvies is seeking permits to do this on every river on the property. It's great for beavers, but it makes economic sense too: over time a property currently covered primarily by pine forests and arid bushland will contain more areas of lush grassland and hardwood trees. That will open up more opportunities for grazing, fishing and wildlife spotting, which are already part of the offering at Silvies.

This long-term vision permeates everything that Silvies Ranch does: things are built to last – not just for years, but for decades. There are nice touches everywhere at Silvies, like naming each course after the previous frontier inhabitants of the land, with accompanying background on their life and times. So too, the custom metal-work across the entire property, including bunker rakes with two- or three-word messages etched into them (my favourites are 'nice polo' and 'you're screwed'). If I was engraving a message to future golfers out here it would have to be 'how's the serenity?'. Because out here, I feel like Darryl Kerrigan at Bonnie Doon*.

*Apologies to our non-Australian readers for this gratuitous and highly colloquial reference to 90s Australian cult movie *The Castle* (well worth a watch).

Interview with Dan Hixson

Dan Hixson is the course designer for Silvies Valley Ranch.

Interview & Photography by William Watt

What was the biggest challenge in making a reversible course at Silvies?

DH: There are many challenges when working on a course like Silvies, mostly due to the remote location. This means that there is a lack of labour force, more limited communications and more time spent away from friends and family during the summers. Plus, converting the natural, rough and wild landscape into playing fields.

What are some of the benefits of a reversible layout in terms of design process, maintenance and resort management?

DH: The design supports sustainability in golf, which is of course very important to the philosophy and mission at Silvies Valley Ranch. It creates two unique layouts within the same footprint of land, utilising less resources.

What is your general philosophy towards course design?

DH: I know this is a cliché, but I always try to focus on fun, and balance that with excitement and challenge. For new courses I like to work with the natural features of the land that would make for unique golf – I am lucky to have been able to work on a property like Silvies that allows me to do this. I am certainly more minimalist and only try to make grading changes when the site requires it. The more I can leave the natural grades as is, the benefits are realised through construction, grow-in and savings to the owner.

I also do a lot of remodel work for a wide range of clients, from simple courses to high-end country clubs and everywhere in between. Therefore, I have to be flexible and adaptive to design and build golf features appropriate for the given project needs and budgets. I love that element of my business as it is in some ways more satisfying to provide a well-designed and -built project at a course that normally would not receive quality design. I often learn in the creative process of trying to stretch the budget more so than working on well-funded projects.

What is your biggest skill or asset as a course designer?

DH: I think it would be the flexibility I try to have, which allows me to create appropriate designs for any type of course or situation.

I think this comes from my background in the game of golf and never having worked for anyone else. By growing up in the game and being a club professional prior to design, I have perhaps a different view of course design. Even though I am self-taught I have been thinking about course design since my youth. It seems there are a large number of designers and architects that tend to design the same as their former boss or mentor. I also think this flexibility allows me to be open to unique ideas from outside sources. A good design idea is a good design idea, regardless of where it comes from. Being able to recognise that someone else may have an idea that is better than my own and figuring out how to incorporate it leads to a good project, and that's more important than who thought of the idea.

So far you've specialised in Pacific Northwest designs – what makes this area distinctive in the world of golf?

DH: The Pacific Northwest has incredible diversity in land, weather, vegetation, climates and quality course in all different types. I have built courses on the coast in thick forest, on ancient sand dunes with 70-plus inches of annual rain, and I have built on desert at 4800 foot elevation with sage brush and 7 inches of annual rain. I have worked on sites in the mountains, near wetlands, next to rivers, around ponds and in grassy meadow valleys. I have built a course with zero trees, and I have worked on courses with over 4000 trees on the property. The Northwest has everything except courses with warm season grasses. Maybe that is why I think being flexible is one of my best assets!

What are some locations you would love to work on outside of this region?

DH: I would enjoy designing anywhere on sand. Like so many of my peers, this is the ultimate. The playability of the turf and drainage are great, but the construction opportunities and the creative options are endless, especially around the greens. I have played in Australia and New Zealand and I would not hesitate for even a second given a chance to design there.

Golf and Comedy

When you're next killing time at your local course – walking between holes, perhaps, or imbibing at the bar – ask your companions to name the greatest golf movies of all time.

Words by Luke Buckmaster
Illustration by CJ de Silva

One title is guaranteed to be name-dropped again and again. *Caddyshack*. Director Harold Ramis's rambunctious 1980 comedy captures the misadventures of bumbling staff and well-heeled clientele at an elite American country club. It's a hijinks-splattered tournament movie with memorable performances from a big cast, including legendary funny men Rodney Dangerfield, Bill Murray and Chevy Chase.

But the best golf movie of all time? That's a big call. It's also one you'll find that has been backed up by countless 'best of' lists published over the years, so the jury is in: *Caddyshack* is widely considered the greatest cinematic hole-in-one.

Watch the film today and it returns mixed results. There are numerous laugh-out-loud moments, including a memorable battle between a dim-witted greenkeeper (Bill Murray) and a meddlesome gopher. Also the scenery-chewing presence of Dangerfield, clothed in a ridiculous rainbow-coloured jacket and armed with an endless number of zingers. It is also shambolically written, haphazardly paced and wildly inconsistent. Harold Ramis lurches between setups and punchlines, delivering plenty of flat spots and shanked gags. If you're planning a re-watch, best to keep your expectations low.

But the prominence of *Caddyshack* in the canon of on-the-green classics is fitting simply because the film is full of jokes. If that sounds like a simplistic reading, its beloved status actually says quite a lot about the way golf has ingratiated itself in screen comedy over the years (and vice versa). Has any other sport, in the history of cinema and television, been mined for laughs more often?

There are several good reasons why golf has lured screen humourists. But first, a potted history lesson in the artists who pioneered the space and used golf to hit comedy sweet spots.

Charlie Chaplin was one of the first. In 1921, playing his trademark character, The Tramp, the silent era superstar sauntered onto the green and created havoc in a film called *The Idle Class*. Mostly his shenanigans comprised simple visual gags involving dunderhead behaviour: accidentally displacing the position of balls when he walked, for example, or taking swings at other people's. Many of Chaplin's contemporaries followed suit. So many, in fact, golfing tomfoolery can be found in the work of virtually all mega-popular American comedians of the 1920s and 1930s, including marquee names such as Buster Keaton, Fatty Arbuckle, Laurel and Hardy, WC Fields, Larry Semon and The Three Stooges.

This early endorsement of the sport's capacity to make audiences laugh had enormous flow-on effect. Work in golf-as-means-to-guffaw was continued in decades to come by too many artists – and in too many productions – to name. Performers include Bing Crosby, Bob Hope, Dean Martin, Jerry Lewis and Leslie Nielsen.

Golf also made its way into many cartoons (including those starring Donald Duck and Goofy) and hugely popular TV shows such as *The Honeymooners* and *The Beverly Hillbillies*. And – more recently – *The Simpsons*, *Seinfeld* and *Jackass*, with about a zillion pit stops in between. In recent years movies with golf course–set jokes or set pieces include *Sideways*, *Johnny English*, *50 First Dates*, *I Love You, Man* and *Hall Pass*.

One of the most famous comedy routines of the 20th century didn't involve the sport at all: Abbott and Costello's seminal baseball-set two-man dialogue exchange *Who's On First?* The crux of the routine relies on humorous wordplay (the name of the player on first base is Who, which causes confusion when the question 'who is on first?' is repeatedly asked). The essence of the routine has nothing at all to do with baseball, the choice of recreation largely incidental. Comedic depictions of golf, on the other hand, tend to rely on elements fundamental to the sport – and this in turn helps explain its longevity on the funny field.

The first and most elemental is the uncluttered look of a golf course. 'It's just nice to be outside in a well-landscaped area,' Jerry Seinfeld once joked. There's some truth to that in an on-screen sense, and also a comedic one. The country club–style aesthetic presents a generally clean visual layout that emphasises the presence of actors and props. The green performs like a stage, where alignment of props and bodies – things that are key to slapstick – can be co-ordinated in an open space.

Certain items tend to be returned to for comedic dividends again and again, most commonly (and unsurprisingly) clubs and balls. In 1930's *The Golf Specialist*, WC Fields takes a swing only to realise the club he is using is bent ridiculously out of whack. Fields plays around with his shoes, his hat and his club; in a twenty-minute film not once does he properly connect with the ball. Goofy had similar troubles in 1944's Disney cartoon *How to Play Golf*. The cartoon character takes a swing and accidentally hits himself in the face. Later, he takes another swing so powerful it spins his body around in circles. The Three Stooges were (unsurprisingly) also rather clumsy when they attempted the sport in 1935's *Three Little Bears*. A highlight is watching a ball hit each of their heads consecutively – doink doink doink.

Another comedic benefit of pared-back settings where there is little visual stimuli is increased focus on dialogue. Given there are few things to look at, the audience's focus can be steered towards funny conversation. Dangerfield delivered the aforementioned storm of zingers in *Caddyshack,* though there are countless other examples of words put to laugh-inducing effect on golf courses.

In Leslie Nielsen's 1993 direct-to-video cult hit *Bad Golf Made Easier* the comedian implored his students to repeat the credo, 'We don't play golf to feel bad, we play bad golf to feel good.' In the 2004 film *Sideways* Paul Giamatti hilariously loses his cool after his uber-calm companion accidentally winds him up by offering unhelpful quasi-sage advice.

Underpinning many jokes about golf is socioeconomic-oriented ribbing that takes aim at the sport as a recreation perceived to be undertaken by snobby (and easily offended) players. Sometimes this manifests as fish out of water–style humour such as a 1963 episode of *The Beverly Hillbillies* where the characters are so uneducated they try to prevent the ball from going in the hole ('I had to stop it or it would have fallen in!').

The premise of Adam Sandler's hit 1996 film *Happy Gilmore* hinges on a badly mannered man-child messing with the system, insulting fellow competitors with crude comments and an uncultivated demeanour. Cruder still was the behaviour of the heehawing team from lowbrow reality TV series *Jackass*, who snuck onto a golf course in 2002 and upset players by blowing air horns while they were in the act of swinging.

These forces of disruption don't have to be human. Donald Duck in a 1938 short film, *Donald's Golf Game*, was infuriated by a bird happily tweeting from its nest above him. And, bringing us back to where we began, in *Caddyshack* that impish and elusive gopher was a source of much frustration, ultimately leading to the demolition of the entire golf course.

In that possibly-greatest-ever golf comedy, Ramis samples many different techniques. Jokes involving visual layout, slapstick, props, dialogue and mocking the elite are all there. Thus the film acts as a kind of golf-comedy compendium. In a sense (perhaps, a generous one), *Caddyshack* is a history lesson in the sorts of jokes that have long appealed to screen humourists. Also the kind that will no doubt draw their attention for a long time yet. ⛳

The Sandbelt

MELBOURNE
·   ·
AUSTRALIA

It's a triangle, a corridor, a belt, a region, a destination and an icon. Few, if any, in the golfing world have ever gone a round without overhearing at least one vaunted spiel about Melbourne's infamous Sandbelt.

Words by Cameron Hassard
Photography by William Watt

←

Above the 2nd hole at Metropolitan Golf Club. World-class golf in your backyard.

Deep in the suburban fringes of a city famous for a number of things – coffee, cosmopolitanism, and notoriously changeable weather – is the region's unique vein of sandy loam subsoil that continues to grip golfing punters from all corners of the playing world.

What defines the Melbourne Sandbelt? That's long been a source of energetic debate amongst golfing boffins. While some dote on the geological, or geographical, others err on the spiritual, the historical. Whatever the perspective, one thing endures: it's a pretty special place to enjoy a round.

THE BEAUTY OF THE BELT

On the surface, the Sandbelt is a family of eight championship courses in Melbourne's south, host to prestigious events including the Australian Open, Australian Masters, World Match Play Championship, Women's Australian Open and Presidents Cup (all of which rank in the top 100 courses in the world). There are also seventeen additional public and private courses – all worthy in their own right, though the top eight usually hog the limelight. Tiger Woods once called the region one of his favourite places to play (suffice to say, it wasn't just the AUD4.32 million appearance fee talking).

Why all the rage about this sandy hub? It's as much to do with what's beneath the surface as above it; so too, the historical vibe that coats the region like a golden halo – most of the Sandbelt's championship clubs are, or near to, a century old, and with unique geology in the mix, the Belt remains, as it has been for a very long time, an enduring hit with the pro, and non-pro, stick-swinging crème.

THE LAY OF THE SAND

There's no Belt without the Sand. Beneath its surface, the Sandbelt comprises a triangle of sandy subsoil, located along Melbourne's southern Bayside outskirts, which extend from the Moorabbin area to the Mornington Peninsula, east to suburban Springvale and Dandenong, and west to the shoreline of the Port Phillip Bay.

The particular variety of sandy soil is considered a virtue in the golfing world: it's good for year-round play; bunkers can be constructed wherever a course designer chooses, without requiring carting in additional sand from an external location; it's excellent for drainage; and bunkers can be cut right on the edge of a green, an impossibility for other courses of different soil varieties. It's hard to beat sand – as Tom Doak agrees in *The Anatomy of a Golf Course*, fifteen of the world's top courses are built on the stuff.

Given the hooting and the hollering, you'd be forgiven for thinking that Melbourne was the only place on earth that lays claim to such a geological anomaly. While there are others, there's nothing quite like this Sandbelt, yet much of that has to do with the 'above surface stuff' – its design influences and its unique lineage.

THE SANDS OF TIME: ROYAL MELBOURNE AND BEYOND

The year 1891 was a big one. Naismith invented basketball. Tesla unveiled his coil. Karl Elsener built the first Swiss Army knife. In chilly, grey St Andrews, the 31st Open Championship kicked off without a hitch.

Down Under, the Melbourne Golf Club – later, the Royal Melbourne Golf Club – was founded. Golf had been played in the Melbourne metropolitan area since the 1840s, but this marked the area's first serious world-class course of its kind. Located in Caulfield (a suburb in Melbourne's south-east), conditions in hindsight were not ideal: potholes and road breaks, and the ever-present hazard of poisonous snakes.

A gold rush city at heart, Melbourne thrived throughout the latter 20th century and into the next, booming in population. This rapid urbanisation led to a succession of location shifts for the Royal

Melbourne Golf Club (a trend that would become common for Sandbelt courses throughout the decades to come, to the present day).

In 1908, the second major Sandbelt site was created, what we now know as the Metropolitan: born of the Royal Melbourne's old Caulfield site, later shifting further down the Belt to nearby South Oakleigh. The Royal Melbourne, meanwhile, had shuffled to the nearby bayside suburb, Sandringham, then to Black Rock, a site perhaps most famous for its West course, designed by the inimitable Scottish course architect Dr Alister MacKenzie.

MacKenzie was the maven of his era, a spearhead of what most consider the Golden Age of course architecture. It's the Royal Melbourne's affiliation with MacKenzie through the mid-1920s that continues to drive its heritage appeal, as well as that of the broader Sandbelt. (MacKenzie's legacy was also enshrined in the design of the nearby Victoria Golf Club, his 1926 bunkering report helping generate a particularly high and enduring positional standard.)

MacKenzie's influence can't be understated here – his design nous single-handedly raised the bar of the burgeoning Sandbelt's playability to a world-class calibre that would last through to present day (all this before he'd even seen his future watersheds at Augusta National and Cypress Point).

And so, from the 1920s on, as the game of golf became ever more embraced, with ample cheap land up for the taking across Melbourne's south, the Sandbelt blossomed with each future championship course: Woodlands, Kingston Heath, Yarra Yarra, Huntingdale, et al. And while clubs felt the tension and pinch of the Great Depression through the early 1930s, they recovered in the post-war 1940s, finding their feet to evolve with ever greater improvements and transformations.

THE MODERN DAY

As Anne Court, former president of the Golf Society of Australia, once put it, 'the outstanding feature of the Sandbelt is the imaginative use of the neutral terrain complete with extensive bunkering'. So too the grandeur of its wide, open fairways, the native eucalypts, the extensive greens, the indigenous vegetation and native plantings.

Today, the region continues to thrive – a proud family of courses admired from near and far – basking in acclaim, yet somehow remaining unusually accessible and affordable (not to say these courses are open to anyone, but unlike equivalent clubs in the US or Japan where only the ultra-elite are afforded a round, the Sandbelt's courses are usually playable through a club member or official introduction to an official, and a waiting list. So too, the fees are worlds apart from the exorbitant rates seen in other countries).

As the beloved Belt creates more and more world-class golfers, and continues to capture the imagination of the golfing world near and far, it remains a sandy wonder world that everyone, it seems, wants a piece of.

The Sandbelt: A Course Guide

Course architect Mike Cocking takes us through the Golden Age in Melbourne, with a rundown of his Sandbelt favourites.

Renderings & Hole features by Mike Cocking
Photography & Course overviews by William Watt
Course layouts by Lie + Loft

When asked to name a favourite golf course designer, the name that invariably comes up is Alister MacKenzie. Even to the weekend hacker MacKenzie's name is familiar. Yet to those who grew up playing around the courses of Melbourne's Sandbelt, it's a justifiable response: the Scotsman, who achieved fame with courses such as Cypress Point and Augusta, came to Melbourne in 1926 for a whirlwind ten-week visit, an adventure that would change the direction of Australian golf forever.

MACKENZIE'S MAGIC

Far away from the links of Scotland, course design was rather primitive in the New World at the turn of the 19th century. This isn't to say there were no great holes built – but these were often based on the famous holes of the UK, which would become known as templates and were used extensively. Many of the original designs suffered from being unnatural in appearance and were too often designed around the principle of penalising poor shots and rewarding straight hitting (aka the penal school of design).

MacKenzie and his contemporaries saw the game more as a cerebral test where holes offered multiple lines of play. Hazards were arranged to tempt golfers to play near them in order to open up either a superior approach shot, a better angle, a shorter shot or a more visible approach. This became the basis of the strategic school of design, which championed interesting holes in order to make the golfer think, reward well-executed shots, encourage creativity, and of course to let the golfer have fun playing the game. Their construction style was vastly different, with irregular lines taking the place of the more geometric shapes in an attempt to make features appear as natural as possible.

In 1926 the Royal Melbourne engaged MacKenzie to redesign their course at Sandringham. Here he met Mick Morcom – the finest greenkeeper he would ever come across, a master of construction. They made a formidable team, with Morcom building all of MacKenzie's work in Melbourne and helping to create the distinctive Sandbelt look.

Whether Royal Melbourne saw the benefits to the broader golfing community in sharing MacKenzie's services, or perhaps they simply found a creative way to subsidise his design fee, the club secured a 50 per cent commission for any consulting work they arranged on MacKenzie's behalf during his stay.

MacKenzie moved at an exhausting pace during his ten-week trip, preparing plans for Kingston Heath, Victoria, Metropolitan, Barwon Heads, Flinders, Royal Adelaide, Royal Sydney and New South Wales, along with consulting visits to Pymble, The Australian, Indooroopilly, Royal Queensland, Brisbane, Bonnie Doon and Manly.

But perhaps a more lasting effect would come from the relationships he formed with people such as Morcom and his young son Vern (who would become the greenkeeper at Kingston Heath), and of course Alex Russell, who he would partner with while in Australia. With MacKenzie spending barely two months in the country, it was left to these three to execute the plans, which were generally just a guide and one that they often deviated from. Following MacKenzie's departure, each became architects in their own right, creating significant designs on the Sandbelt, and across the country. Morcom constructed (either partly or wholly) almost all the work that arose from this period of Sandbelt activity – no mean feat when you consider that they also managed to hold down full-time greenkeeping jobs at the same time: Mick at Royal Melbourne, and Vern at Kingston Heath.

The legacy of MacKenzie, so too Morcom, Vern and Russell, endures in the countless examples of premium hole design across the Sandbelt. All who play it have their own preferred holes. Short par-4s and par-3s feature prominently in my short list – while not necessarily the best, these little ones are some of my personal favourites. It's one of the many virtues of the Sandbelt that even its lesser-known courses contain at least one or two world-class examples.

Royal Melbourne: Setting the standard

West: 6077 metres, par 72
East: 6007 metres, par 71
Composite: 6401 metres, par 72

Blessed with the most interesting, undulating land on the Sandbelt and two world famous routings, Royal Melbourne has not sat on its laurels. Leading the way with agronomy, indigenous plant programs, international tournaments (such as the Presidents Cup in 2019) and world course rankings, Royal really is the queen of Sandbelt. Despite all this, it balances a sense of exclusivity and historic weight with a friendly membership base and a freedom of movement that belies its reputation. Whilst the West course gets all the plaudits (and rightly so, it is magnificent), the East course is also spectacular and flies under the radar of the great courses of the Sandbelt.

16th Hole West

Par 3 – 202 metres

In a city with many fine short par-3s, it's perhaps curious that I've put this one as a favourite. However, the 16th at Royal Melbourne might just be the best long one-shotter in the country. Demanding both a perfectly struck shot and a perfectly flighted one in order to find the putting surface, the 16th can be particularly unkind to poor technique and nerves. Any sort of mis-hit or miscalculation won't find the green, generally resulting in your ball tumbling off to the right where a difficult up and down awaits.

Given that most golfers get a shot here you'd think more would elect to play it as a short par-4, using a mid-iron and a short pitch for an easy bogey. However, golfers aren't always known for their clear thinking, and ego often takes over (it's amazing what the number on the scorecard can do).

The advances in ball and club technology have been unkind to holes such as this. At 202 metres, it's still a strong hole, but it wasn't that long ago that a fairway wood or even a driver could be used here, as seen in the match between Peter Thomson and Gary Player in the TV series *Shell's Wonderful World of Golf*. Sadly, to achieve the same today the tee would have to be moved well into the Sandringham Golf Course, which shares the boundary some 70 to 80 metres away.

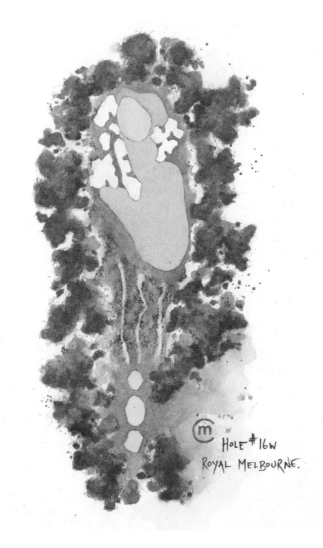

HOLE #16W
ROYAL MELBOURNE.

Kingston Heath: Understated elegance

6800 metres, par 72

Understated and cool yet always welcoming, Kingston Heath sits in the heart of the Sandbelt on Kingston Road. With its single-storey clubhouse full of cleverly designed and relaxing spaces, fresh minimalist branding that evokes its iconic heath flower, some of the best-practice facilities in Melbourne and a course routing that's impossible to get tired of, Kingston Heath is the club of choice for many of Melbourne's true golf lovers. Capable of hosting international championships including the World Cup of Golf in 2016, it's also a relaxing walk any day of the week for members and their guests.

Bordering busy Moorabbin Airport, plane spotters will be happy with the buzz of single-engine craft coming and going. But one's eyes will be drawn back to the course before long – one of the first to embrace an indigenous heathland revival program and with continuing works on sightlines and bunkering, this is a special place to play golf and relax all year round.

←

A shaft of morning sun lights up the par-3 10th hole.

↗

The approach to the brilliant 3rd.

3rd Hole

Par 4 – 269 metres

At only 269 metres it's barely the length of an average drive on the PGA tour, but with a tiny tilted green rejecting anything but the perfect approach shot, the 3rd at Kingston Heath is no pushover.

Unlike many of the world's best short par-4s, the 3rd gave designer Dan Souter virtually nothing to work with. It's flat, the ground is heavy, and there was no obvious green site or natural features to take advantage of. So while the design and the subsequent bunker scheme by Alister MacKenzie was first class, the genius of the 3rd really resulted from its brilliant construction, and to Mick and Vern Morcom we ought to be eternally grateful.

The strategy of the short 3rd centres around its green, which perfectly balances the knife edge between what is interesting and what is fair. It has enough tilt to reward those who have played to the correct position on the fairway, while at the same time inflicting equal punishment on those who are out of position. Judging the ball flight and spin is crucial. With the steep slope from back to front, simply being in the correct position on the fairway isn't enough. The trick is to execute the perfect pitch, with enough flight and spin to stop the ball, but not so much that it runs back to the front of the green.

The fairway is shaped a little like a bottle: wide at the tee end and narrow at the green. Bunkers positioned on the left guard the best angle into the green and everything from a driver through to a mid-iron is a legitimate option from the tee. When combined with the pin position, the weather and your own confidence, club choice becomes all the more confusing – indeed, any time you can put doubt into the minds of the golfer you've done your job as an architect.

HOLE #3
KINGSTON HEATH.

Metropolitan:
Stay sharp

6800 metres, par 72

Metro has long held the reputation of the finest conditioning in Australia, and it's certainly a point of pride to the grounds crew here to maintain that position. But with relatively generous (and flawless) fairways, it's the greenside bunkering that really packs a punch here. They are cut so aggressively into the putting surface, it's not uncommon to see golfers begging their ball to stay on the dance floor before looking to the sky as it rolls off into oblivion. The bunkers, although deep and intimidating, are a joy to play out of with the fine sand asking the golfer to dig in and providing a distinct advantage for locals who have the knack. Host to the World Cup of Golf in 2018 and of many tournaments past, Metropolitan is meticulous about all aspects of the course and facilities, and runs a tight ship. Golfers during the World Cup of Golf needed to be as sharp as the bunker edges here to succeed.

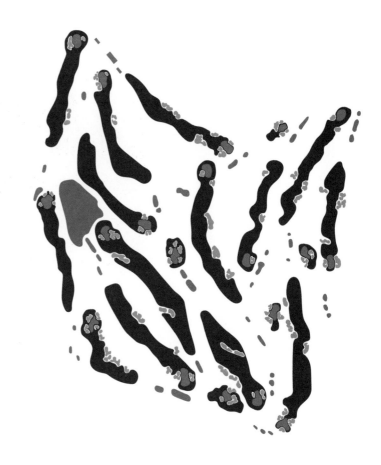

←

Distinctive razor-sharp bunkering and pristine surfaces at Metro.

↗

The approach view for the 5th.

5th Hole

Par 4 – 378 metres

The original Royal Melbourne Golf Club was located in Caulfield, and for the historically minded reader its clubhouse still remains as a private residence (16 Turner Street) in what is now Malvern East. In 1901 the club was wise to react to the pressures of urban growth and decide that much better land was available a little further towards the beach at Sandringham. Half the club agreed with this move while the other half looked elsewhere and settled in Oakleigh to form the Metropolitan Golf Club.

The original designer was another MacKenzie – JB – who laid the course out in 1906. Of course Alister had some influence, creating a design plan twenty years later, which was partly implemented by Mick Morcom after his departure.

The course sits on a mixture of flat ground (predominantly on the back 9) with some nicely rolling dune land on the front that rises to a peak at the 4th and 5th by boundary the course shares with neighbour, Huntingdale. I've always liked this older, more undulating part of the course the most – particularly the medium length par-4 5th. The green is the highlight of this course, with a huge shoulder on the right side helping sling balls toward the left. This can be used to your advantage when playing to a left pin, but when it's on the opposite side, the corner is to be avoided and can really only be attacked by coming in from the left, close to the fairway bunkers.

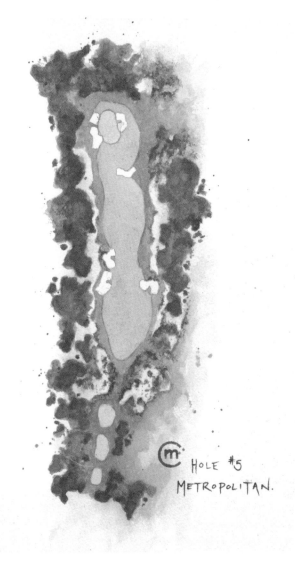

HOLE #5
METROPOLITAN.

Huntingdale:
A modern take

6383 metres, par 72

Home to the Australian Masters (of Gold Jacket fame) for over thirty years, Huntingdale became one of the best-known courses in Australia throughout the 1980s and 1990s. Requiring plenty of length off the tee, the approach shots at Huntingdale demand precision – anything wayward and there's most likely a bunker waiting for you (as the par-3 12th hole, shown below, will attest). Whilst the routing might look up-and-down at first glance, there's a great variety of holes here and, as with all Sandbelt courses, it's a beautiful walk. Huntingdale also boasts a luxurious modern clubhouse and brings a sense of occasion and style to a day on the Sandbelt.

→
Greenside on the 8th.

8th Hole

Par 4 – 314 metres

Huntingdale was the last of the eight Sandbelt courses to be built. Designed in the late 1930s and open for play in 1941, neither the Morcoms, Russell or MacKenzie were involved here. This course was the result of another collaboration between international architect and local superintendent Charles Alison and course curator and architect Sam Berriman.

Alison was once a partner of both Harry Colt and Alister MacKenzie, and built many well-known courses around the world – his best though, perhaps, away from England and in Asia and the US. Whilst he never visited the Huntingdale site (he designed the course entirely from topographic plans), he was fortunate to have Berriman carry out the plans as he was a terrific designer in his own right.

Berriman's par-3 holes and his more heavily bunkered green complexes were some of his best. While they're credited to Alison, I'm sure he influenced more than just the outcomes here. Not surprisingly my favourite hole is the short par-4 on the 8th. The fairway narrows around driving distance with bunkers set on both sides, so the decision is typically whether to lay-up with an iron into the widest section or try and drive somewhere near the green.

The green is the real highlight: raised and angled slightly from front left to back right with a sea of bunkers cut into the sides, making for perhaps the most attractive approach on the course. One of the keys to the Sandbelt is understanding its angles, and when the greens are firm and fast (as they typically are in the warmer months), even a few metres can make the difference between landing in a perfect pitching position or scrambling to make par.

HOLE #8
HUNTINGDALE.

Peninsula Kingswood: A fresh start

South: 6321 metres, par 72
North: 6124 metres, par 72

After nearly ninety years, Kingswood Golf Club closed its doors – a sad day for some of the members there for whom a lifetime of memories are tied to its weatherboard clubhouse. However, with a merger deal struck with Peninsula Golf Club has been born a new super-club for Melbourne golf. With the newly built North course designed by local Sandbelt firm Ogilvy Clayton Cocking Mead (OCCM), early indications are that it's destined for big things. Combined with a grand new clubhouse and on-site accommodation, Peninsula Kingswood makes the Sandbelt's southern-most club a true golf destination.

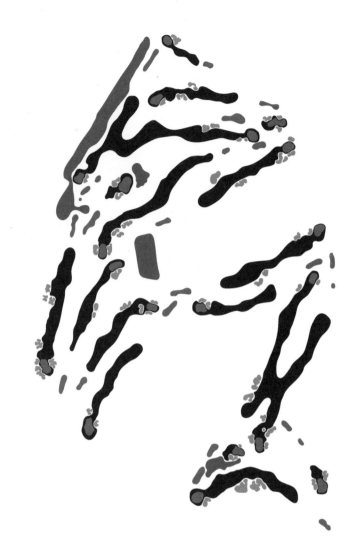

←

The new clubhouse at Peninsula Kingswood, and newly unveiled indigenous heathland species thriving.

↗

The uphill approach to the 6th hole on the North course.

6th Hole North

Par 4 – 320 metres

Travelling from the Sandbelt down to Flinders in 1926, MacKenzie would likely have been miffed to learn that he was within just a few kilometres of the site of the future Peninsula course. What he would have given to get his hands on this spectacular property.

The Peninsula has seen its share of changes over the past hundred years. Originally built as an 18-hole course, which stretched from the southern part of the existing site and down through what is now a residential area, it was converted to the course in the 1960s by Sloan Morpeth, the manager at the Commonwealth. Over the next fifty years, multiple architects, committees and superintendents made changes to each of the courses. None of these have been as significant as the latest project, which has seen the entire site and golf holes redeveloped.

As a junior, I well remember the curious tee shot at the 6th on the North, which forced players to try and hit up and over the trees on the corner. Over the last decade or so, changes have been made to help reveal one of the best short par-4s on the course.

There are a multitude of options from the tee, playing up the narrow section of fairway on the left, firing out to the right side of the 70 metre wide fairway, or playing aggressively over the diagonal line of bunkers. The new green matches these options from the tee with the slight horseshoe green offering pins that need to be approached from one side of the fairway or the other.

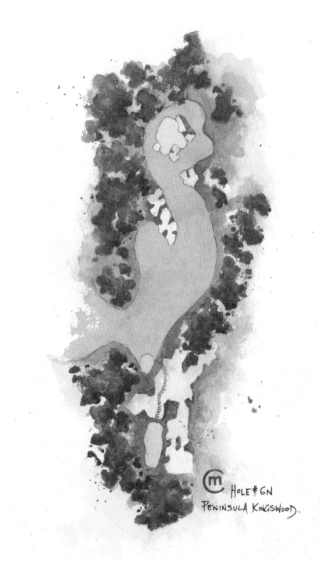

HOLE # 6N
PENINSULA KINGSWOOD.

Commonwealth: Grandeur & beauty

6380 metres, par 73

Commonwealth Golf Club could lay claim to being the prettiest of the Sandbelt clubs – a grand, elevated and classic clubhouse overlooks the 1st and 18th holes, and offers a glimpse of the tree-lined fairways beyond. Making the most of a site that works its way down to a scenic lake on the iconic 16th, Commonwealth presents beautifully year round.

16th Hole

Par 3 – 364 metres

The Sandbelt's only true waterhole is also one of its best. The 16th at Commonwealth is the epitome of a strategically designed par-4 around water. For years, architects have tied themselves in knots adding mounds, superfluous bunkers and rough to add drama to something that needs little help when designed correctly. Here at the 16th the architect created as much variation, options and intrigue as any of the closing holes of a TPC course using just two hazards and a wide band of fairway.

The primary hazard of course is the water, stretched almost the full length of the hole and shaped to create a perfect curve, which tempts those on the tee to bite off a little more of the dogleg than what they're capable of. The wide expanse of fairway to its right is just as essential design-wise, and it's always in the back of your mind to play conservatively.

The green is central to the hole's brilliance. Smallish by Sandbelt standards, the combination of a tilt from right to left and a deep bunker on the right side makes any approach from the right infinitely more difficult than near the water and, of course, the longer the shot the harder it is still.

More than once I'd reached this hole in a pennant match needing a strong finish, only to nervously push a 3-iron out to the right and face an incredibly difficult long iron from a bad angle. To see the best amateurs today hit a driver because they can hit over the water is a sad reflection of the modern game. Still, every now and then the hole gets one back, and thoughts turn to a more conservative tee shot next time around.

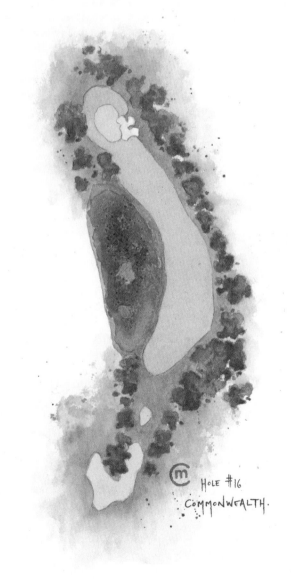

HOLE #16
COMMONWEALTH.

Victoria:
Traditions run deep

6278 metres, par 72

Home to legend Peter Thomson, whose bronze statue overlooks the first tee, Victoria Golf Club retains an old-world charm about it that hearkens Melbourne's boom years. A full renovation of its green complexes (including a conversion to bent grass) under the guidance of OCCM was completed in 2019. Victoria shares a border with its more famous neighbour, Royal Melbourne. The land, however, is just as special with rolling sandy hills host to a thriving collection of native Australian plants and trees and bunkering as good as anywhere on the Belt.

← *The 14th green at Victoria leads elegantly to the 15th tee (right of frame).*

↗ *The 15th is an unforgettable par-4, with the Melbourne skyline also visible here.*

15th Hole

Par 4 – 290 metres

You guessed it: another short par-4. While the 10th West may get all the accolades for drama, given its sizeable landforms and the enormous bunker cut into the hill on the corner, there's a good argument to suggest that the 15th is the better hole.

Rather than being an all-or-nothing tee shot, the 15th has an almost infinite number of options from the tee, which have increased in recent years with further widening of the fairway and tree removal down the left of the hole. Quite legitimately, golfers can play anything from a mid-iron right through the bag to a driver off the tee in order to avoid trouble and to leave them with the best line in, or to try and force a much-needed birdie. Club choice might vary from day to day with a new pin position, a change in weather or wind direction, or perhaps, most critically, your confidence on the day.

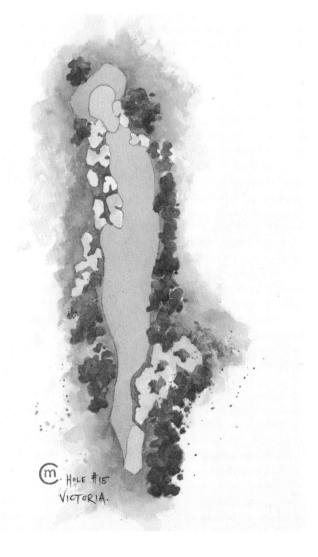

HOLE #15
VICTORIA.

Yarra Yarra:
Hidden treasures

6102 metres, par 72

Recently undergoing restoration by Tom Doak's Renaissance Golf Design, Yarra Yarra is a classic routing by Alex Russell, who worked closely with MacKenzie. The 11th hole, described by legendary Australian golfer and scribe Peter Thomson as a 'national treasure', is generally considered to be one of the best 18 holes in Australia. With its Mediterranean-style clubhouse sitting central to the property, and a grand entrance drive snaking through the course, the relaxed atmosphere at Yarra Yarra is conducive to friendly conversations and a great day of golf.

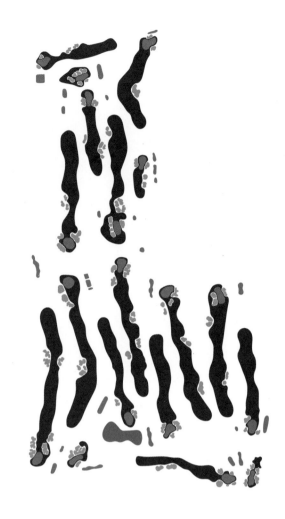

11th Hole

Par 3 – 165 metres

Alex Russell may just have the best strike rate of any designer in history. After assisting MacKenzie with the design of the West course at Royal Melbourne he went on to design just a handful of courses, all of which would become highly acclaimed: the East course at Royal Melbourne; the wonderful and highly underrated links course Paraparaumu in New Zealand; Lake Karrinyup; and, of course, Yarra Yarra.

There are many excellent holes at Yarra Yarra, including the long par-4 5th (possibly its best hole), and the par-5s at the 9th and 16th. But for me, the par-3s here are the most memorable, with the best one at the 11th. This green site is slightly elevated from the tee, which gave Russell (and likely Mick Morcom) an opportunity to cut a dramatic set of diagonal bunkers across the front of the green. The green itself is one of the most wildly undulating anywhere on the Sandbelt, meandering up a series of tiers and ridges from the front left to the back right. The combination of the forced carry and wild green would almost certainly mean that this green wouldn't be built today (not around the Sandbelt anyway).

Play can vary here, from a pitch to the front left pin and front tee, to a longish iron when the flag is in the back-right corner (best attacked with a well-controlled fade – for the right-hander anyway).

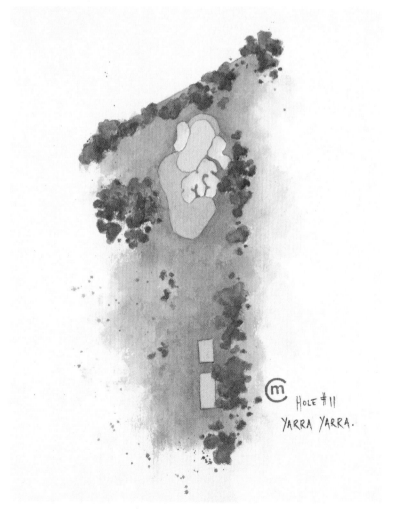

HOLE #11
YARRA YARRA.

Filthy Beautiful

Words by Nicklaus Mills
Photography by William Watt
Illustration by David Baysden

Close your eyes for a minute and let your mind paint a picture of a beautiful golf course. What does the course look like? Does it have lush fairways, defined rough, smooth greens, all framed by a tree-scape or ocean clifftop?

For many, an introduction to beautiful begins the first week in April when the Augusta National Golf Club hosts one of the biggest tournaments of the year: the vibrant pink azaleas, the rich green fairways, the crystal clear creeks all contrasting with Tiger Woods's Sunday red. It could almost describe the scene of a picture, or an evocative painting. Of course, it's worth remembering that beauty – whether in art or on the golf course – remains firmly in the eye of the beholder.

Over the years I've enjoyed hosting golfers from around the world on Melbourne's Sandbelt. I like to share the history and some of the amazing golfing moments that have happened on the same fairways (and occasionally, the same tea tree – like Greg Norman's scrub-laden nine shots that cost him the Victorian Open). Some of these golfers have acquired deeper knowledge and understanding of the Sandbelt. Yet many others never really know what to expect as they drive through the gates of these courses. Their desires and expectations have been based largely on the course ranking and they automatically assume an Australian adaptation of Augusta National.

For those in the know, the Sandbelt is a wonderland of a slightly different ilk. Not beautiful in the common way, but what I like to describe as filthy gorgeous.

Guests will often begin by playing their first Sandbelt holes in a somewhat hesitant fashion. As we meander along the fairway I like to explain that it's just like playing golf on a Monet; this is often followed by looks of confusion. What I mean by that is that they're playing golf of a different type of artistic style.

Just as Andy Johnson from The Fried Egg podcast refers to the parallels between golf course architecture and music genres, one can parallel golf course architecture to fine art. Throughout the ages, art styles and movements have changed, reflecting an artist's own expression and influence viewed through a different lens. This principle follows golf course architecture and design – after all, how can you compare the links of North Berwick to the desert fauvism of Wolf Creek in one realm? Art styles create categories, not hierarchies of importance.

Take a course like Sleepy Hollow, which I would parallel to the style of cubism. Its geometric greens and bunkering are balanced with loosely flowing fairways. A plan view of the 15th hole earmarks Picasso's *Weeping Woman*. In contrast, a drive two and a half hours south brings you to Pine Valley, which emulates romanticism: a heightened interest in nature and an emphasis on the individual's expression, emotion and imagination.

Pine Valley could be the apotheosis of the Golden Age of architecture. It is a collaboration of the greatest architects in one period, all working together to create a course that far exceeds reality. One of the artworks I admire most is Eugene Delacroix's *Liberty Leading the People*, which perfectly captures the French Revolution in one piece. The 18th hole at Pine Valley strikes in a similar fashion, perfectly capturing the closure and total essence of the course's design.

And the Sandbelt? I see French impressionism. At Kingston Heath, I see a Monet. In this style's infancy, French impressionism faced enormous criticism that the movement wasn't artistic enough. This

movement, despite controversy, began to push a more conceptual boundary, the intention being to capture a feeling and an experience in a precise moment with the light dictating the artwork. To capture the moment, Monet would paint multiple pieces (around twelve) in one sitting. Similar to Kingston Heath, where it captures a million precise moments as the course constantly and subtly changes over time. It can look different from morning to afternoon, winter to spring, and decade to decade.

There is also a level of subtlety to the beauty of Sandbelt golf. Recently I went out in the late afternoon, trying to squeeze out the remains of the day's sunlight. Standing on the 4th green at Kingston Heath, which lies central to the course, I looked across the heathland towards the 6th green, the closing hole in tournament play, framed by the silhouette of the clubhouse. The last of the amber light and the pink hues reminded me of Monet's *Houses of Parliament*. The indigenous vegetation in between the holes played on the vision of Monet's rough brushstrokes and the afternoon's

amalgamation of light gave me the Monet moment that is unique to Melbourne.

Almost none of the courses on the Sandbelt use the borrowed landscape. All of the views and vistas are internal, with subtle doglegs hiding and revealing certain views. The greens host the best views, sometimes showing where you came from, where you will go, and occasionally, in golf architect and writer Michael Clayton's words, 'holes that aren't holes'. Enjoying this kind of beauty is similar to impressionism: its initial impact doesn't have the easy and commercial attractiveness that some of the courses in the golfing world have. The more we understand and appreciate the beauty in different styles, the more we begin to change the perception of what is beautiful. Perhaps there will be a progression in golf course architecture away from cookie-cutter courses that follow the monotonous and synthetic beautiful design, to courses that provide more Monet moments and leave us forever with indelible impressions.

←
Artist David Baysden's take on the Sandbelt aesthetic.

Silk Upon
Sand Dunes

NORTH ISLAND · NEW ZEALAND

Links enthusiasts around the world are salivating at Tom Doak's offering on the New Zealand coastline, Tara Iti.

Words & Photography by William Watt

The first time I saw the flowing, wall-to-wall fescue at Tara Iti my jaw dropped. The stunning contrast of the perfect fairways with the rough, barren surroundings, its muscular form highlighted by the late afternoon light, was something to behold. The air of expectation that had been building to this final stop on my trip was immediately justified. There's no question that Tara Iti is an extraordinary experience.

There is an unmistakable air of exclusivity and palpable energy as you enter the gates at Tara Iti and see the first traces of manicured green amongst the pines that remain from the original plantation, which was largely cleared during construction of the course. Famously designed by Tom Doak after he spent 'four days wandering around the forest and walked out with a routing', the auxiliary elements that go into a destination course are equal here to the course architecture. The reception area conjures images of a Bond film: the desert-like landscape enhanced with subtle buildings and minimalist landscaping. Even the staff uniforms, combined with a sort of serene but friendly attitude, seem to fit with the other-worldly vibe.

Tara Iti was conceived by American investor Ric Kayne. He had run a few potential sites past his preferred architect, Tom Doak, before settling on a pine plantation just a few miles north of Mangawhai Beach – a quiet, friendly coastal town that sees an influx of holiday-makers from nearby Auckland during the summer months. From the start, expectations were high, recalls Doak. 'Mr Kayne only wanted to build the course if it was going to be really special, so on our first site visit, the operative question was whether I thought we could build one of the best courses in the world. Having worked on a couple of those, I appreciate more than most people how many things have to go right along the way to get where he wanted to go.'

It's clear a lot of things went right here. Out on course, it's immediately clear that Tara Iti is more like a giant work of art than a humble golf course. Miles of flawless fescue roll through the dunes like pure silk, guiding the player through the alien landscape with a surprising ease and a sense of meant-to-be-ness the way it hunkers into the landscape. The ultra-minimalist course furniture (which consists solely of locally sourced stones used as tee markers) combined with greens that melt into fairways and bunkers that blend into sand dunes make for a disorienting experience. A lunar lander cruising past with an astronaut offering a friendly wave wouldn't be out of place.

This state of confusion is something that Tara Iti's Caddie Master, Steven MacDonald (Stevie Mac), believes is important to building the caddie–player relationship at the course. 'I was asked, "When can we have markings on the sprinkler heads? When can we have GPS involved?" I didn't want any of it on the golf course. I felt, to give the caddie program a chance and to ensure we could enhance the skill level of the caddies, embracing simplicity of design was important. So yes, it's a minimalistic approach to golf course furniture, course markers, tee markers and so on. It's raw, but it's exciting to see the landscape as it is, and to feel a little lost in the dunes is something quite special without signposts of where to go next. Often the golfer is a little disorientated and it's like "where the – where do we go next?", and our caddies can guide them to the next tee, which is often in a surprising location, so it's an adventure.'

It also helps to explain why Tara Iti has decided to make caddies a mandatory part of the playing experience – the only course in New Zealand to do so. Functionally, it simply works a lot better for golfers to have some guidance. But as MacDonald explains, a caddie program means a lot more to a player's round than just navigating the course. 'There's no doubt the interaction with our caddies forms a huge part of the experience. I think that's one of the most enjoyable things is that combination of our membership and the caddie program coming together and creating new friendships. It's my job to manage the member and the caddie, and try to unite them in a happy marriage. We always say to our caddies "enjoy yourself out there" because it feeds into the player's experience. Even if the player is having a bad day, I want my caddies to have a great day, because eventually they'll buy into the energy.' Sourcing 80 per cent of his caddie team from the local area is also an important way for the club to give back to the local community; they're conscious of the negative image a billionaire-backed, exclusive membership club might present. MacDonald explains: 'For such a special piece of land and a special golf course, we've gone to the local schools and local golf programs here and we've attracted age groups ranging from eight to fourteen [years], fourteen to twenty [years], and stretching out a little bit further to universities. We're encouraging them to get a little bit of pocket money, to learn a new skill, and make some connections, which may help them in later life.'

Course architect Tom Doak is also conscious of golf's reputation as an elitist sport, but maintains there is a place in the game for projects like Tara Iti. 'Golf exists right across the demographic spectrum. New Zealand is full of affordable country courses where people get out and enjoy the game – the game in New Zealand is generally much healthier than in the US, though it's the American-financed, expensive resort courses that get all the attention in magazines. But there's certainly a place for something like Tara Iti too, and it can have a great impact on other NZ courses. When we were down there a year ago for an event, my caddie for three days was Leo Barber, who's the superintendent at Paraparaumu, New Zealand's other best links course. And I guarantee you that Leo saw a few things at Tara Iti that will give him ideas to go back and make Paraparaumu that much better for his members. Likewise, the pro at Titirangi, Doug White, has become a good friend, and one of my

younger associates who worked on Tara Iti, Clyde Johnson, is now doing some consulting work to improve Titirangi. So the fact that Mr Kayne funded Tara Iti can have a positive impact on a larger scale.'

There's certainly knowledge to be gained from working with the experienced team from Doak's Renaissance Golf Design. Despite Tara Iti being picture perfect today, it took all of that experience to wrestle the difficult site into shape. Doak explains: 'It was clearly a special site, but once we started clearing the trees away, we were completely engaged in battling the elements to get the course built. The entire site had to be cleared and revegetated with native dune plants, and getting all of that established before the wind changed our shapes was a difficult job. My associate Brian Slawnik spent two and a half years in NZ fighting the winds to make it look like it had always been there. It's really one of the most difficult jobs we've ever done, and it's a great compliment to my crew that most people don't recognise that. Most seaside courses are volatile and windy sites, especially on sandy terrain because the uncovered bits tend to blow around and build up at the edges. We worked closely with the superintendent CJ Kreuscher throughout the project, and we've encouraged him to roll with the punches. From here out it's the opposite problem, keeping the native plants from overtaking the landscape! We want people to be able to find their ball in the sand and play it, and he's going to have to keep hacking away to preserve that playability.'

←
The pristine white sands of the North Island coast are a perfect canvas for links golf.

→
If there's a better looking golf course on earth, I'm yet to see it.

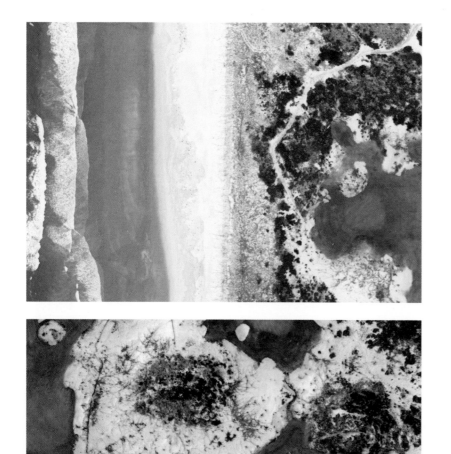

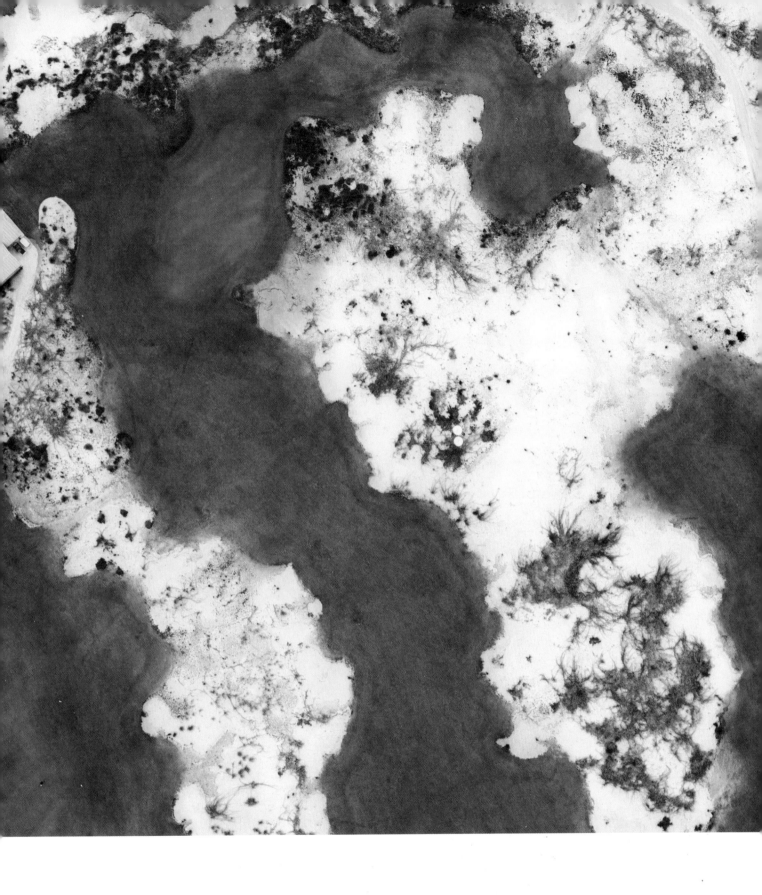

Bone Valley

FLORIDA

•   •

U.S.A.

Built upon former mining land in a Floridian locale, Streamsong is an unexpected golfing paradise. With bold, almost audacious design by three of the world's leading course design firms – this is modern destination golf at its grandest.

Words & Photography by William Watt

←

The opening hole on the Red course makes it obvious this is somewhere unique.

↙

Tee view of the par-3 6th on the Red course.

After three hectic, eye-opening and buoyant days at the PGA Merchandise Show in Orlando spreading the word about *Caddie Magazine*, I hit the road for Streamsong, a resort boasting the area's three hottest golf courses. The approach to Streamsong, about one and a half hours' drive south of Orlando, builds some intrigue after leaving the main highway: long, straight, flat, narrow side roads traverse over clay and rock, crisscrossing a railway line and dodging hundreds of small lakes. Known as Bone Valley for the large collection of fossilised remains found throughout the region, this entire area was covered by ocean in prehistoric times. Amongst the layers of sand and rock, bone fragments from prehistoric sea creatures, such as the megalodon – a terrifying 80 foot shark – are regularly found. Being a former seabed littered with fossils, the land is subsequently rich with phosphate, one of the primary crop fertilisers used worldwide. Which is where the Mosaic Company – the world's leading producer of concentrated phosphate – and the visionary behind Streamsong, Richard Mack, come in.

The process of mining for phosphate in Central Florida is not a subtle one. A form of surface mining, it involves a massive digger pulling back the top layers of sand and soil to reach the phosphate-rich layer of sediment below, which is then pulverised into a slurry and processed offsite. The land left behind after the mining process is usually a series of huge sand dunes, and – given Florida's tropical climate – geometric lakes. The mining company, in this case Mosaic, is then tasked with returning the land to nature, which typically involves planting trees and creating wetlands environments. However, Mosaic's founding executive Richard Mack had a better

idea. 'I played collegiate golf and have great respect and passion for the game. Mosaic has been in the phosphate-mining business in Central Florida for more than a century. Once we complete mining in an area, we typically reclaim it back to its original form. Rather than doing that, I felt that we could do something different and innovative with our land – use the dramatic landscapes to create a unique and special golf destination. I was influenced by the incredible topography of the land: dunes, native grasses, elevation and sweep. Our sand features are amazing, and sand is a common denominator of the world's best courses. Being in the mining industry for decades in this region, it was also a goal to create economic vitality in an area that could use the boost. So, that was the inspiration behind how Streamsong originated, and it snowballed from there.'

Now that it is built and thriving, Mack's idea seems like a logical one, but at the time that it was conceived in 2007, it seemed like a long shot. Just as other destination resorts like Bandon Dunes were starting to hit their straps, the global economic crisis hit, and the golf industry felt it harder than most. 'It was an interesting time to be advancing the notion of a new golf resort, in Florida, nonetheless,' says Mack, with a heavy dose of understatement. 'Sometimes decisions like this seem like they are inopportune from a timing perspective, but if you think about it, we were about the only big play that was advancing at that period of time, which helped on the marketing of the project. The anticipation of Streamsong in the golf world was palpable when we ultimately opened in 2013. When we started this project there was a dearth of new golf construction, so everybody in the industry was very eager, to put it mildly, at the possibility of working on this project. The selection of architects was critical, and obviously we partnered with Bill Coore, Ben Crenshaw and Tom Doak – amazing people.'

This dream team of architects were tasked with working in harmony and, as they'll admit, in friendly competition with each other, on a parcel of land considered reasonably tight for 36 holes. Whilst calling it a codesign would be going too far, the creation of Coore and Crenshaw and Doak's Renaissance Golf Design certainly involved collaboration during the routing process to ensure both the Blue and Red courses made the most of the available land. The two shaping teams then went to work adding the distinctive features which define each architect's design practices, while always keeping an eye on what the other team was up to. The results of this collaborative work are truly spectacular, which is somewhat unsurprising given the highly unusual canvas such a talented group were given to work with. And though I can't wait to take a divot on those two courses, it's really the Black course by Gil Hanse, built on the success of Red and Blue, that brings me here.

BLACK COURSE

As Streamsong began to attract more and more of the burgeoning golf tourism market, rumours of a third course were running hot in the golf architecture community. Mack describes the 'tremendous interest' he received as he approached the commissioning process in 2014. As with the two founding courses, Mack knew what he

wanted, and Gil Hanse and associate Jim Wagner were always in the frame to win the job. The timing for Hanse, soon after the announcement of winning the bid for the Rio Olympic course, couldn't have been better. As he describes in an interview with *Caddie Magazine*, 'As far as I know we were the group that they were focused on. We met on several occasions with Richard Mack. Jim Wagner and I walked the site to get a sense of it prior to our selection. The client offered us several parcels to choose from and we did some preliminary routings on a couple of them to ultimately come up with the layout for the Black course. As you can imagine, this was a much sought after commission, so we were pretty exhaustive in our exploration of the sites to find what we believed to be the best course.'

The site they chose, directly south of the existing courses and separated by a low-lying wetlands area, is massive: almost comparable to the entire site of Red and Blue, and covered entirely with fine white-grey sand, not dissimilar to Melbourne's Sandbelt region. Of this comparison, Hanse agrees it was part of their thinking. 'We felt that if we referenced the bunkering style of the Melbourne Sandbelt it would be a point of differentiation between our feature work and the work on Red and Blue. However, our biggest point of reference was from a playability standpoint, as we opted to grass the surrounds of the greens with the same type of grass that is on the greens. This has caused some confusion from players who are not used to seeing Sandbelt or links courses where the grass in the surrounds is maintained for playability and not for

colour differentiation. It was our hope that this presentation would allow for the ground game to be a prominent part of the recovery options for golfers around the greens. It has taken some getting used to, but we are hearing that players love the way it plays even if they are not used to the way it looks!'

Indeed the look of the course is quite unique – large expanses of the aforementioned bright sand, contrasted with muted tones of fine Bermuda grass covering bubbly topography. Comparisons to Mammoth Dunes at Sand Valley (designed by David McLay Kidd), are inevitable. But the grandeur here is a little more nuanced, and there are definite design and branding nods to Tom Doak's incredible Tara Iti in New Zealand. The experience offers that same other-worldly vibe as Tara Iti, minus the serene setting. Whilst the Black course is front and centre of the in-vogue trend of expansive, bold but playable design, Hanse says that the style came out of the land itself, rather than any specific philosophy. 'It was a combination of three elements that led to the expansive style of the course. The client wanted us to build a golf course that would be able to host any possible tournament, and that leads to needing length for the competition and space for all that comes along with a tournament. Secondly, Jim and I believe that width is a key element to creating a playable golf course for all of us average golfers, while still making angles relevant for golfers who are trying to post a score. Finally the site was large and we felt that the features and scale of the course needed to match the scale of the property.'

After being given his first look at the available property in 2014, Hanse and his team of 'cavemen' were on-site by the end of 2016, having decided on a routing that would complement the existing courses but be distinctive in its own right. Asked if there was added

pressure to follow the work done on Red and Blue, Hanse is both confident and respectful. 'We viewed it more as an opportunity for us to be able to put our work side by side with the designers that we respect the most in the business. We felt that the differences in our site from Red and Blue would provide enough of a contrast that our course would be considered complementary to them, as opposed to feeling pressure to create something to compete with them. Stylistically I think a lot of parallels can be drawn between our work and the work of Bill (Coore) and Ben (Crenshaw for the Red) and Tom (Doak for the Blue), however, their courses were purposely commingled and occupy a more intimate scale as they relate to each other. Our course is off by itself, and by its sheer size and scale we knew it would feel different from the other two, and it would hopefully add another element to golf at Streamsong.'

As part of a media crew invited down from the PGA Show to experience the course, my playing partners and I are treated to an excellent lunch at the striking Bone Valley Tavern prior to the round. Designed by Alfonso Architects, the Black clubhouse sits elegantly and harmoniously on the land, playing an important part in forming the identity of the course. The restrained palette of materials includes the use of *shou sugi ban* (Japanese charred timber cladding), and slender steel window frames which allow for views through the dining room to the landscape beyond. The strong rectilinear form provides a striking contrast to the aforementioned organic white sands and sweeping fairways of the course.

After fully shanking twelve consecutive shots at the driving range, I'm a tad nervous heading out on course; although not as nervous as my caddie, Peter 'Rabbit' Horrobin, who after discovering during the round that I am not completely awful at golf, later describes the range session as 'crazy'. However the par-5 opening hole quickly gets my attention off the range session. A semi-blind tee shot, strategic second and the first look at the oversized green complexes has the whole group engaged immediately. The 2nd and 3rd are both strategic and tough par-4s that offer a tantalising glimpse of the upcoming holes. The massive, valley-jumping par-5 4th offers an enticing risk-reward choice for your second shot: at 600 yards from the tips, the green isn't in play for all but the Rory or DJs of the world, but a good second shot back over the valley will offer a far easier wedge in than a more timid approach, which would leave the valley clearance until the third shot.

While my playing partners putt out at the terrific green complex, I take a glance over at the upcoming 5th and wow, that's a big bunker! Falling away to the right of an elevated green, it's the biggest raked bunker in the world reckons one of the caddies. It's hard to argue with him on this one. Fortunately, the green will take anything hit up to 30 yards left of that bunker and feed it in nicely to a back-right pin, which proves to be something of a trend throughout the course. As an Aussie I can occasionally be uncomfortable getting a caddie but without the very chill Peter Rabbit on the bag for this one, I would have regularly underestimated the extent of slope and feed onto the green from strategically utilised dunes, sometimes up to 30 or 40 yards from the pin. The gigantic, muscular punchbowl green on the 9th is unlike anything I've seen before – it must be 80 metres across. We spend a few minutes just rolling balls around the edges of the thing to see it in action; the blind approach means you don't get to watch how your shot fares on the various humps and slopes.

The vibe in our group is noticeably buoyant on almost every hole – the course seems to offer a lot of 'members bounce' moments, where a little nudge in the right direction will perk up someone who might be struggling a bit. There are bad breaks too, but never disastrous, and there is terrific variety and strategic interest on every hole. At least three of the par-4s take the driver out of your hand, something that doesn't happen as often (at least for me) on Red or Blue. Hanse agrees that it's an important part of his and Jim Wagner's design ethos, but the process to achieve this is more free flowing than you might imagine.

'We work very hard to come up with variety in the layout of the course on paper during the routing process. However, where this really comes to life is in the field where we work with our shapers or associates, the cavemen, to add another layer of variety in the shots required to play the holes. This next level is what we are truly very conscious of. We are constantly comparing and contrasting the elements of each hole we build, to make sure we do not fall into a repetitive pattern. This continual editing process in the field is what we believe to be the only way to achieve the variety and balance that's so important in golf course design.'

Things get a little more narrow around the back 9, with the par-5 12th demanding accuracy on all three shots in. Hole 13, rather uniquely, has two pinnable greens which make a left or right decision on the snake-like centreline bunker important to get right. The drivable par-4 14th and gap-wedge par-3 15th are a favourite stretch for our group, with birdies starting to flow readily. Hole 17 is a cool par-3 with a water backdrop, before the awesome par-5 18th takes us home around a lake. As the last group out for the day, by the time we get to the 18th tee it's actually dark; but somehow my playing partner Megan and I find our drives, get on in two, and two-putt for birdie by phone torchlight. Birdies in the pitch dark is a great way to finish our first round on the Black.

← The giant punchbowl green on the par-4 9th on the Black course is something to behold.

→ Rustic minimalist furniture adds to the vibe at Streamsong.

BLUE & RED COURSES

Over the next couple of days between photography and beer sessions, I'm lucky enough to play the Blue and Red courses in calm, early-morning conditions. Both are world-class courses and provide a slew of memorable holes. From the 100 foot high 1st tee on Blue, perched at the top of a dune, it's clear this is a course that is going to test your heroics; all too often I'm tempted to play the riskier shot, such is the allure of pulling it off. The par-3 7th is the hole in all the photos, and with good reason – it was just meant to be there. As with any Doak design, nothing looks out of place, and the questions never stop being asked.

The opening 7 and closing 4 holes on Coore and Crenshaw's Red course are some of the most distinctive, memorable and fun on the entire property. That's not to say that the holes in between are weak – not at all – but weaving your way through the unnaturally steep dunes and serene lakes is what truly sets Streamsong apart from any other golf experience in the world right now, and these holes amplify that aspect the most. The genius of the routing is, again, that every hole seems to sit as it should, yet the variety is endless and the scenery just beautiful. The Red course is a slightly easier walk than both Blue and Black, taking advantage of more subtle variations in elevation through well-placed tee boxes within the many dune complexes. The show-stopping Biarritz green on 16 has to be seen to be appreciated in full, and the strategically excellent but gettable 17th and 18th make for a finish that's hard to forget.

The Red course was the pick of a very fine bunch for me. It could have been a number of factors external to the course itself that led to that conclusion. My score helped – but it was the charming couple from Cleveland, Earl and Berle, both in their mid-eighties, that made the experience so enjoyable. Watching them potter around the course and marvel at every aspect of it (the trip was a treat for Earl's 84th birthday) whilst rarely hitting it more than 100 metres kept a constant smile on my face.

All three courses deserve their places on the various world-ranking lists, and you could make an argument for any one of them outpointing the other on a given day (something that many were doing in the various 19th holes around the resort). It's clear that this was a project executed with a passion for golf in mind, and a clear desire to let the top architects in the game flex their design skills. You'll just have to play them all.

→

The par-3 5th on the Black course is a heroic hole featuring one of the largest raked bunkers in the world.

The Arnold Palmer

Words by Dave Carswell

Illustration by Jo Murphy

The age-old debate: was it one third lemonade to two parts iced tea or fifty-fifty? Could it have been two thirds lemonade to one third iced tea? Does anyone care? The contention around Arnold Palmer's own preferred ratio was equal to the muddied history of how ordering an 'Arnold Palmer' came to be part of the mainstream lexicon. The popular (and slightly more romantic) version has the birth of the drink at the 1960 US Open, in Cherry Hills, Colorado, which Palmer fittingly won. However, the King himself brought some more clarity to the tale by more recently confirming that the name of the drink was born in Palm Springs sometime later in the 1960s after a long hot day of golf course design work. Upon hearing him explain his favourite concoction to a waitress, a nosy table neighour overheard his order and requested an Arnold Palmer.

A remarkable hallmark of his charisma and allure was the desire of men wanting to be him and women wanting to be with him ... and wanting to drink like him. The naming of the drink also validates the depth of his celebrity status that the single ordering incident sparked a wildfire of requests to the point where eventually bartenders at sports clubs around the US knew exactly what the order entailed. Whilst Palmer wasn't the first person in history to combine the refreshing allure of iced tea with the sweet and tart mouthfeel of lemonade, his status as a sporting icon helped shift the drink to cult-like status, national popularity and eventually a multimillion-dollar beverage company. However, much like his reluctance to be referred to as the King, he also showed remarkable humility in rarely using his name when requesting the concoction made in his honour. A true sign of his gentlemanly stature and humble reluctance with fame. As for that ratio? If Palmer was still alive today, I am sure he would instruct you to pour it however you see fit. ⛳

Links Among the Vines

BORDEAUX
•   •
FRANCE

Pardon the interruption, but Bordeaux is about more than just wine. A stronghold of the French golf scene has emerged, and may just prove to age as well as a bottle of the local vin rouge.

Words & Photography by William Watt

←

The ancient town of Saint-Émilion features ancient Roman ruins and vineyards of a similar vintage.

G olf isn't the first thing that comes to mind when travelling to the Bordeaux region. Far from a links paradise, this is the world's epicentre of wine, and the locals certainly aren't afraid to claim that title. But it wasn't really wine nor golf that brought me here on my honeymoon with my new wife, Rosie; it was more a sense of exploration and curiosity at what this up-and-coming yet historic city has to offer. After some last-minute research into attractions in the area, I had learnt of a recently opened Tom Doak course nestled among some of the oldest and most famous vineyards in the world. Suddenly our three-day schedule looked quite busy as I began to line up a round, with hopefully minimal disruption to the honeymoon and my very understanding wife.

Setting out of Bordeaux the next day in predawn light, the classic, immaculate forms of the châteaux (large, historic country houses with vineyards) showed that wine is, as it has been for a long time, the big show here. Even the vines themselves, perfectly manicured year-round, exuded a sense of significance and confidence. As we meandered through back roads dotted with these estates, staff were already arriving to roadside camps to tend the vines, and uniquely skinny tractors, no wider than the Frenchmen driving them, proved an amusing obstacle.

As with anything as old and influential as wine from Bordeaux, politics has played a major role in the distinct classifications of these châteaux. The Bordeaux Wine Official Classification of 1855, a system requested by Napoleon III, is still in play and has barely changed since its inception. Deciphering why the various levels

of *crus* (or growths), from *premier crus* to *cinquièmes crus* (fifth growths), have been awarded is almost impossible today – despite changes in land ownership, head winemakers, and everything else involved in the wine business, the same list from 1855 prevails. Each subregion in the area also has its own classification system, resulting in many court challenges and disputes, such is the value ascribed to each level of classification.

But all of this melted away like a hangover after a strong coffee and several pain au chocolat, as I manoeuvred the car through the flat, almost marshy-looking land east of Bordeaux, first through the Entre-Deux-Mers region ('between two tides', owing to its position between two tidal rivers) and then into the Libournais, where the rolling hills really kick in. The first grapes were planted here by the Romans as early as the 2nd century, and there are châteaux that date back to the 1200s still producing wine today: a palpable history that lingers around every corner of the undulating, vine-covered countryside.

THE GRAND SAINT-ÉMILIONNAIS GOLF CLUB

One town in the heart of the vineyards north of the Dordogne river, Saint-Émilion, has been the international face of this region for centuries, having been the first Bordeaux appellation to export its wines to other countries. Today the entire town is listed as a UNESCO World Heritage Site, owing to beautiful cobblestone streets and a series of religious sites built over the centuries. One of the oldest is a limestone church in the centre of the village,

←

A patchwork of
vineyards in the heart of
Bordeaux.

→

Beautiful poster designs
from the Trophée
Lancôme.

established by the town's founder, a Benedictine monk who was known as Émilion. Émilion lived in the area until his death around 767 AD, spending his years evangelising the local population who later named the town in his honour. It's not clear whether he drank wine or not – but either way, that seems to be his main legacy, with most of the town now given over to wine merchants, restaurants and tour companies promising an insider's view of the notoriously hard-to-access vineyards.

Another fifteen minutes' drive through the never-ending vines, we arrived at a plot of land that has remained strangely vineyard-free over the centuries, and was claimed by the prominent Mourgue d'Algue family in the early 2000s. The pioneering elder statesman of the family, Gaëtan, has dedicated his life to the development of golf in France, and could be compared to a sort of French Arnold Palmer. During the 1960s, Gaëtan purchased a struggling French golf and tennis magazine and rebadged it *Golf Européen*, running it for many years as the primary golf publication in France. He later convinced his friend, chairman of Lancôme Pierre Menet, to establish the Trophée Lancôme – a tournament that attracted some of the biggest names in golf at the time, including Gary Player, Lee Trevino, Seve Ballesteros and Arnold Palmer himself (who won its second staging in 1971). The beautiful advertising posters created for these tournaments now adorn the clubhouse at the Grand Saint-Émilionnais Golf Club, the latest of five courses that Gaëtan has created over his lifetime in the game. The entire d'Algue family has helped to bring the club to life, including Gaëtan's son, André, who helped unearth the site and was instrumental in attracting Tom Doak to bring his design genius to the project. André's wife, Philippine, looks after marketing for the club, and his sister, Kristel,

a former US College player and European Tour winner, lends her communication skills and considerable golf talent to the operation. Not to be outdone, their mother, Cécilia, holds an incredible forty-five amateur French Championship titles, continues to win senior tournaments and is a charismatic presence around the club.

The vision for the course was to bring together the philosophy and skills of these multiple generations to create an experience that embraced the French l'art de vivre, or art of living. This included creating a course with a light touch on the land, an immersive and challenging playing experience, and a welcoming and relaxed clubhouse environment.

Tom Doak was commissioned to design the course after André sent a contour map to him in 2011. According to André, 'Tom got back to me right way and said he was interested. A few months later he came and spent two weeks in the Saint-Émilion area and decided to go ahead.' I asked if Tom was encouraged to take on the project with the help of the incredible array of local wines. André smiled. 'Perhaps one or two glasses.' Once the project was underway, Doak devised the routing in a matter of three or four days. The team were immediately impressed with his approach. 'He didn't follow the obvious path. Previously there had been some trees cleared on the property that had created several sightlines we thought he might follow. But he completely went against that – it wasn't even in his thinking. And then, magically, the site opened up and created this scenario whereby playing the course is a journey of discovery. There are surprises at every turn. It was really a special thing for us to watch his genius shape the site during that time.' Over the following four years, Doak and his team from Renaissance Golf

XIIIème TROPHÉE LANCÔME

21, 22, 23, 24, OCTOBRE 1982, GOLF DE S^t NOM LA BRETÈCHE

PARIS   ORGANISATION: GOLF EUROPEEN   FRANCE

9eme TROPHÉE LANCÔME

19, 20, 21, 22, OCTOBRE 1978, GOLF DE S^t NOM LA BRETÈCHE

PARIS   FRANCE

PALMARES: 1970 TONY JACKLIN (GB)-1971 ARNOLD PALMER (U.S.A)-1972 TOMMY AARON (U.S.A)-1973 JOHNNY MILLER (U.S.A)
1974 BILLY CASPER (U.S.A)-1975 GARY PLAYER (AES)-1976 SEVERIANO BALLESTEROS (ESP)-1977 GRAHAM MARSH (AUS)

10eme TROPHEE LANCOME

25, 26, 27, 28, OCTOBRE 1979, GOLF DE S^t NOM LA BRETÈCHE

PARIS   FRANCE

12ème TROPHÉE LANCÔME

15, 16, 17, 18, OCTOBRE 1981, GOLF DE S^t NOM LA BRETÈCHE

PARIS   FRANCE

Design made minor changes before settling on the final routing. Doak had plenty to work with – the site, a former forest and hunting area, has quite dramatic elevation changes throughout, with this northern bank of the Dordogne River known for having a more interesting topography than the flatter southern bank.

THE COURSE

The opening tee shot, within putting distance from the clubhouse, is downhill to a generous landing area; however, only one half of the fairway offers a good line into a relatively sedate, bunkerless green. The 2nd is a tight and tricky short par-4, with the first sighting of a creek that runs throughout the property to be avoided. In fact holes 3 and 4 both cross the creek, before the uphill par-5 5th takes us up to the highest point on the course and fantastic views of what is to come on the back 9. Holes 6 through 9 feature native gorse and wildflower areas, quite distinct from the rest of the course, which has more of a parkland character, with old-growth oak trees and pines lining most fairways. Just when you think you have seen the whole property and are ready for the stretch home, the 15th takes you in another direction, falling down towards a neighbouring creek to another secluded corner of the course. It's a cracking hole, with vineyards behind the tee, a generous landing area for your drive and then a strategic second shot required to get a look past some dramatic green side contours.

The 16th – formerly the most difficult hole on the course as a long par-4 that played into the prevailing wind – has been slightly lengthened to a two-shot par-5, presenting a late birdie opportunity and creating the unusual finishing sequence of par-5, par-5, par-4, par-4. A nice feature here is the view of a 16th century church up on the hill, deliberately carved out through clever tree removal, creating a distinct memory of the hole as well as a target for the approach shot.

The bunkerless 17th is one of the best on course, with a gentle dogleg left rewarding those who take the long way round – cut the corner too much and you're left with a much smaller target than from just 15 yards to the right side of the fairway, which opens up the green beautifully.

The 18th brings you home with a fairway-splitting bunker requiring a deft (or lucky) tee shot, before an uphill approach towards another excellent green complex – views across the valley's vineyards beyond the driving range are a bonus.

With just 35 bunkers on the course, the design work is beautifully understated, and each hazard is in play and of strategic importance. As with any course Doak puts his name to, this will become a destination for many travelling golfers, but it's been built with members in mind and there is a great sense of a small but passionate community here. With plans for an extensive clubhouse renovation on an imposing Edwardian to complete the playing experience, the Saint-Émilionnais Golf Club will sit comfortably and proudly among the endless manicured vines.

I returned to Bordeaux that afternoon after my round to find Rosie had compiled a rather frightening list of restaurants for us to try before our scheduled train to Paris the next day. Even the most discerning foodie will never be bored here: the service, menus and overall quality are as good as anywhere in the world, and the wine lists are mind-boggling. Where Lyon had been full of incredible produce and authentic dining experiences, Bordeaux added a layer of polish (and euros) across the board. But in the end, the best meal we had was a simple picnic in the city's garden comprised mainly of wine and cheese, as we watched the locals embrace l'art de vivre.

←
Kristel Mourgue d'Algue tees off alongside the vineyards.

A Journey into the Arctic Circle

LOFOTEN

·　　·

NORWAY

Photographer Jacob Sjoman's first visit to the Arctic Circle yielded an album of rugged beauty and spectacular skies. The remote fishing archipelago of Lofoten has built a spectacular golf course, and oh, how it glows.

Photography by Jacob Sjoman

Land of a Million Pagodas

BAGAN

•   •

MYANMAR

Buddhist temples and golf rarely cross paths, even though some golfers could probably use some meditative qualities in their game. In Bagan, you'll find a golf course that sits in harmony among the pagodas and temples.

Words by Jane Knight
Photography by Jane Knight & Paul Arps

First light flickers through the window and stirs me from a broken sleep. I wake to the surreal view of vast planes, with the occasional historic stone pagoda. It's worthy, I decide, to wake the others and I reach around with a quick nudge. I also feel a sense of relief as it confirms we're on the final kilometres of our overnight bus haul from Yangon.

Located in central Myanmar, on the east bank of the Ayeyarwady River, lies one of the most significant archaeological sites in South East Asia. This is ancient Bagan: a glimpse of an incredible legacy left over by a devout Buddhist population over 1000 years ago.

Formerly known as Pagan, the first capital of the Burmese kingdom rose to its height during the 11th century under the monarchy of King Anawrahta. The king's hubristic nature and desire to seed Buddhism across the country resulted in the building of thousands of elaborate pagodas. While King Anawrahta's reign fell short when he fell in the path of a water buffalo, his dynasty continued for over 200 years. Over 2200 pagodas still stand today – hundreds restored to their former glory, many mid-transformation, others relatively untouched – a remarkable landscape that remains one of the most significant Buddhist pilgrimages in the world.

We quickly discover that each pagoda was designed to be unique. Stepping inside reveals hidden surprises: 8 metre tall gold leaf-clad Buddhas, ancient scriptures on crumbling stone, and hidden passages that lead to pitch-black staircases and ascend to stunning rooftop vistas.

We enter one at dusk with nobody else in sight. We pass through the entrance, arched with vibrant pink and purple bougainvillea, and are instantly surrounded by darkness. I'm a moment behind and when I enter, the others have disappeared. Listening to the sound of muffled laughter I can make out which direction to move in. I feel my way around the walls and up a spiral stone staircase, eventually towards the light. Without knowing it from the ground, we've found ourselves in the heart of the archaeological zone, with magnificent 360 degree views of pagodas laid out in every direction.

The Dhammayangyi Temple is one of the most popular to climb at sunset, the long shadows of the structures casting themselves over the land, eventually disappearing. Here, toward the north-east – as the relics become sparser – there's a modern watchtower, somewhat of an eyesore amidst the otherwise ancient skyline. This tower belongs to the Amazing Bagan Resort, home to Bagan Nyaung Oo Golf Club, laying on the edge of this incredible archaeological field.

GOLF IN COLONIAL BURMA

During the 1800s, three wars between the Burmese and the English over a period of sixty years resulted in British colonisation of Burma in 1886. With the region annexed as a province of British India, it was sometimes referred to as the Scottish colony due to the heavy role played by Scotsmen in the region's colonisation.

Unsurprisingly, golf was introduced during this period. As depicted so meticulously by George Orwell in *Burmese Days*,

the clubhouse became the centre for social gatherings during the British occupation. It was a popular place for senior staff of trade organisations, officers of British Regiments, ranking British administrators and merchants to meet and talk business.

The sport became increasingly popular – yet remained exclusive, played by military top brass and the super-rich – with more clubs being established around the country. By the 1920s golf had taken root in the colonised territory, even as Burma's intelligentsia, Buddhist monks and the Students Union at Rangoon (Yangon) University waged their first protests against British rule. This uprising included Aung San (father of Aung San Suu Kyi), who eventually led Burma to independence in 1947 before being brutally assassinated by an opposition group.

GOLF IN MYANMAR TODAY

King Anawrahta left thousands of ornate pagodas; the British left golf courses. There are now over 120 courses across Myanmar, in varying quality after decades of neglect under the junta regime. Many are close to Yangon, including Pun Hlaing Golf Club, designed and built by former South African pro Gary Player. This 7100 yard, 18-hole course in the north-west of Yangon is considered Myanmar's best course and nicknamed the 'Pride of Myanmar'. The land – formerly a 650 acre rice paddy – holds magnificent views of the Hlaing and Pun Hlaing rivers, along with the spectacular backdrop of the city and the remarkable Shwedagon Pagoda.

The course has not been without controversy. Gary Player received unfavourable attention in 2007 when former archbishop Desmond Tutu backed a call by his fellow Nobel Peace Laureate and Burmese opposition leader, Aung San Suu Kyi, for an international boycott of foreign companies doing business in Burma, in order to place pressure on the military regime. Tutu also called for Nelson Mandela to withdraw an invitation for Player to host a charity fundraising tournament due to Player's business ties with Myanmar, condemning the course as 'a playground of the ruling junta in the murderous dictatorship of Burma'.

Player, who has raised millions in support of underprivileged education through his charity foundation, maintained that 2002 (when the course was built) was a time when the world's relations towards the regime in Burma had thawed. Aung San Suu Kyi had been released from house arrest, and many believed the country was on the cusp of real political change. Unfortunately, in 2003 Aung San Suu Kyi's house arrest was reinstated and the military maintained the power they had seized in the 1964 coup led by General Ne Win.

It was during Ne Win's dictatorship that the country's name was changed without consulting the population. As pro-democracy demonstrations grew in 1989, they were met with stronger resistance from the junta, and suddenly what was known globally as the Socialist Republic of the Union of Burma became the Union of Myanmar. Many, both in local conversation and international relations, continue to refer to the country as Burma as a statement against the brutal regime, however, over time Myanmar has slowly become adopted.

A ROUND AT BAGAN NYAUNG OO

The Bagan Nyaung Oo Golf Club might lack the polish of Player's course, but wandering between ancient pagodas offers an unparalleled experience. Our caddies Mo Mo and Gi Gi greet us dressed in club uniforms: long khaki pants with a light green jacket and a broad-brimmed straw hat. They both wear squares of *thanaka* paste on their cheeks, which is commonly seen on the faces of women and children in Myanmar. Derived from the thanaka tree (*Murea exotica*), the paste is believed to have anti-ageing properties.

The 18-hole course features tight and sometimes unforgiving fairways, flanked each side by acacias, palms and cedar trees, and a thick floor covering to ensure Mo Mo and Gi Gi earn their wage.

Their endearing giggles suggest they are perhaps used to caddying for a more practised golfer.

The greens are well maintained by female groundskeepers who water and weed by hand. The fairways accurately reflect the dry zone in which the region is located, but you can be confident your ball will find a tuft before you reach it, perhaps a foot or so from its lie, thanks to the caddies. The 4th and 6th holes have you teeing off next to or toward pagodas, and putting out on the 7th comes with an unsurpassed backdrop of the archaeological zone – ruins and palms scattering the horizon.

This skyline is just a small slice of the rich and diverse history that has played out in this ancient place. Remarkably, new chapters of atrocity are being written less than 200 kilometres west of Bagan today: the humanitarian crisis against the Rohingya people, which many are referring to as genocide, has warranted Desmond Tutu and Aung San Suu Kyi to again correspond in the hope of restoring peace.

The 8th and 9th holes weave back to the clubhouse without too many surprises and at 10 am the heat is climbing, as are our thirsts. We've taken to the local Myanmar Beer, one of the tastiest local beers in Asia, and a perfect way to end the round.

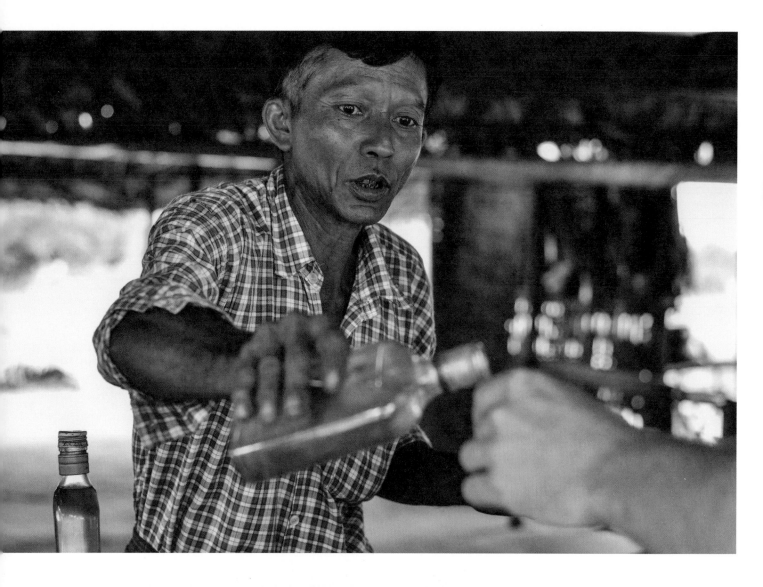

Burmese Beer

The history of alcohol consumption in Myanmar dates back centuries. With sanctions lifted since the end of the junta years, the local beer scene has seen some big changes. Myanmar Beer still owns the largest market share, however new global entrants such as Heineken and Carlsberg have crept in, while the country's first microbrewery, Burbrit, opened its doors earlier this year with a solid range of European-style brews.

It quickly became a daily ritual for us to settle into one of the many open-air beer stations and sample a cold one with the locals. One of the traditional tipples is toddy (htan ye), or Burmese beer (or 'sky beer' as some locals affectionately call it). While it's difficult to come across in the cities, it's still the preferred drink of farmers and workers in the rural areas, especially in central Myanmar.

We stopped in at Toddy Bar as we were leaving Bagan. Under the low thatched roof, a man wearing a longyi greeted us and showed us to a small table and a circle of stools that had, along with the hut, been crafted from palm leaves. Here we heard about the physical exertion required to capture the palm sap that toddy is derived from.

Farmers select the mature male palm trees and men known as tappers rig up a ladder of sorts, tightly tied to the thin trunk of the approximately 100 foot palm. They scale the tree with a couple of pots and a machete tied at the waist. Once at the top, the tapper will slice a cut deep into a palm frond and hang the pot below to collect the dripping sap overnight. The tapper heads back up the tree the next day to collect the full pots. The time of day the sap is captured at determines the strength of the self-fermenting drink, with an afternoon collection resulting in a stronger style.

The sap is then simmered over flames until it takes a sugary solid form known as jaggery, which then spends a couple of days in a ceramic vat mixed with water and sticky rice, where it continues to ferment. The mixture is then poured into pots over flames to be distilled. An iron wok is placed on top, and cold water is continually poured into the wok, which creates condensation underneath; this eventually drips into a sloping tube which delivers the liquid into a glass bottle.

We were served a glass of toddy with a plate of assorted seeds and nuts. As you can imagine, it's a fairly strong drink holding a sweet and nutty aftertaste. Perhaps it was a little too early in the day for us to really enjoy it, so we chose to stick to the Myanmar Beer from that point on.

Birdies, Barrels and Brownies

Words by Reece Witters

Illustration by David Baysden

The weatherman relays that there's been a big dumping of rain in the hills. The water levels will be on the rise in the local rivers and streams, transforming them from gin clear to chocolate milk. The brown and rainbow trout will hunker down and won't feed until the water clears, ruling out fly fishing for a handful of days at best. He says the southerly is expected to turn north-easterly by the weekend, but assures that it's the last of the rain for the time being. A brief look at the SwellMap app confirms what I already knew, that a meaty swell is on the way. When that southerly turns offshore I'll be pitted deep in some barrels by Friday.

Tuesday arrives and it's a bluebird. It's crisp – 17°C expected – but that southerly requires a second layer. Everybody converges on the links – surfers, fly anglers and golfers as one; today being the perfect day to tee it up. The links serve as the ideal meeting ground for seaside, back-country and urban folk. Everyone's welcome, we're all locals, we're all golfers today. The connections are strong; there are no weak links.

So what draws us all to the manicured turf with our quiver of sticks? Is it the same thing that draws Kelly Slater to the tee? That pulls Jack Nicklaus and his fly rod to the back-country rivers in New Zealand? And takes Rafa Cabrera-Bello to the best surf breaks he can find while hopping between the PGA and European tours? There are no shortage of examples where these three popular codes overlap, but is it possible to put a finger on what exactly hooks us deep in the jaw like a well-presented Royal Wulff? Let's look a little deeper into the water.

One of the greatest golfers of all time, Walter Hagen, was fascinated by the sport of fly fishing after admiring the fly casting of some experts in his local area. The flamboyant Hagen saw synergies with golf, and believed his putting touch and feel for timing should make him equally skilled in fly casting. He noted the timing of these experts, specifically 'the manipulation of his left hand on the line ... I could easily understand how timing and precision handling of the rod and line were relative to the timing and hesitation at the top of the golf swing'. The golfing hall-of-famer fell for the idea of becoming an expert fly caster. The hook had been set.

Greg Norman, whose nickname 'The Great White Shark' is derived from his love of the ocean and surfing, didn't start playing golf until he was sixteen. He was too busy waxing his board and paddling out off the coast of Queensland. Norman loved the individual pursuit aspect of surfing: 'You on a board, and that board against Mother Nature.' During his early experiences of surfing, Norman now believes he was inadvertently training his body with certain things that applied beautifully to the game of golf – incredible core strength, stability, narrowing his focus and making sure his body was in the right place at the right time.

It comes as no surprise that Norman developed a strong friendship with surfing GOAT Kelly Slater. Norman and Slater have been known to share intense conversations about the affinity between golf and surfing. The eleven-time World Champion Slater has also taken the route of surf-to-turf, claiming to peg up about 150 rounds a year. The Californian casually sports a three handicap and regularly features in Pro-Am fixtures such as the AT&T at Pebble Beach and the Alfred Dunhill Links Championship at St Andrews.

Perhaps the sweet-swinging Adam Scott was eavesdropping on conversations between The Shark and the Salty GOAT? Also a fond ocean lover, Scott is not only the first Aussie to win the Masters, he's also the first surfer to sport the Green Jacket. Go figure.

For European Tour fans, Ken Brown should need no introduction. Five Ryder Cup outings for Team Europe as a player, plus an appearance as Vice Captain. These days, the affable Scot is one of the most renowned voices in European Golf. Brown describes golf as the 'fulcrum' to all the good things that have happened to him in his fruitful life, including teeing it up with kings and presidents. However these days, the aptly named Brown loves nothing more than stalking brown trout in rivers and streams at unrevealed locations across the United Kingdom. A keen ear for European Tour commentary will pick up friendly fire between Kenny and American Jay Townsend about the virtues of dry fly fishing versus Jay's stoic nymphing technique.

Examples and stories of high-profile golfers who fly fish, surfers who golf and golfers who surf are as plentiful as the waves crashing on the golden sand Down Under. But it's not exclusively at the sharp end of the game where we see these three pursuits overlap. My very own local golf club is a great example. I come from a sleepy little surf town renowned for its variety of quality surf breaks – and its lesser known but equally impressive access to quality back-country water for fly fishing. Our proud club rests on a sporty links track with a modest membership. A big number of the members, and local visitors to the club, are avid fly fishermen, and the club is underpinned with an unmistakable surfy vibe.

Recently I joined up to play a few holes with a windswept older fellow at my course who was firing at flags with only seven sticks in his quiver. Turns out he was a mad-keen surfer who chased waves year-round. His motto: 'When the surf's low, I go and shoot low.'

However, it was his humble opinion that even the most hardcore golfer who surfs will choose to surf over golf every time if the surf's up. Golf will always be there when the swell isn't, he ensured. Surfers tend to bring an 'I'm here to make shots, not count shots' attitude that translates to a creative and relaxed approach to the game. They're all about the early wave, afternoon 9s, 'throw the pencil away' kind of golf that's infectious and fun to be around. Shakas brah!

Across town, New Zealand's recently crowned Fly Fishing Champion Cory Scott has hung up his net following another record-breaking season, closing the loop on a decorated competition career. Scott's pathway is notable given the competitive surfing he enjoyed during his grommet years; surfing was his number one passion before he headed inland to the rivers. While fly fishing became his main competitive outlet, the world of surfing is how he earns his crust. Scott now owns *New Zealand Surfing* magazine, after an extended period as the chief photographer and content director. The talented Kiwi has lapped the globe countless times watching the world's best surfers carving breaks at close range behind his lens.

There's no denying the strong connections between these three pursuits. All are soulful experiences with opportunity for strong artistic expression, requiring healthy doses of courage, balance, patience and creativity. Golf, surfing and fly fishing are all considered difficult to master and hard to perfect: sports that in many ways you cannot clock or complete, yet they offset steep learning curves with unrivaled reward and satisfaction. Outdoors amongst the natural environment, these sports are dependent on uncontrollable natural factors, and all typically take place at the margins of seas, rivers and land. But are we any closer to agreeing what binds these codes together like inseparable siblings?

Perhaps it's that perfectly delivered cast, a fully-loaded line shooting purposefully from the rod tip toward the submerged shadow you saw rise moments before. The line falling delicately onto the surface, careful not to splash and spook the fish, the dry fly parachuting down behind and kissing the top of its intended target. Then the anticipatory wait as the current drifts your imitation snack into place for that hungry brown trout.

Maybe it's a purely struck long iron, held up against a right-to-left breeze with a purposeful fade that penetrates under the stiff southerly. The ball cleverly dropping just short of the intended target and rolling up neatly under the hole, leaving only a few feet uphill for a makeable birdie. You remove your putter cover and enjoy a long walk toward the dance floor.

Or could it be seeing the sets form in the distance while you instinctively paddle toward your intended take-off zone, the manoeuvre into your sweet spot while anticipating the effect of the offshore breeze? The seconds spent calculating what the moving currents are likely to do as the approaching shadows grow darker. The thrust of momentum you get, the plan that comes together as you find yourself locked in a glassy barrel framed by a crystal chandelier.

Whatever it is, there are similar unanswered questions. What's around that last point break? What does this dogleg reveal? What's beyond that deep pool? It's that search for more, the desire to learn, the curiosity of the unknown, the craving of adventure. One more hole, one more wave, one more cast. Because we're all the same – we're here for the adventure of what's around the bend. Whether it's birdies, barrels or brownies. ⚓

Conquering the World's Longest Golf Course

OUTBACK

· ·

AUSTRALIA

Spread across 1365 kilometres of the remote Australian outback lies the world's longest golf course. Not for the faint-hearted or the fly-averse, the Nullarbor Links is a challenge of mind, body and spirit.

Words & Photography by Dave Carswell & William Watt

←

The Nullarbor includes the longest stretch of straight road in Australia.

'I only ever stop if there's a golf course. If there's no course, we just keep driving.' For someone who has just driven 2500 kilometres, retiree Kerry's well-timed introduction not only serves to prove his dogged intent, but provides a catchcry for what will unravel over the following days. Kerry is in town to play the Nullarbor Links, perhaps the world's most peculiar golf course, and definitely the longest. The course was conceived by the Eyre Highway Operators Association as a way to encourage travellers to stop in at the various roadhouses and towns along the prodigious outback highway stretching from Adelaide to Perth. More imaginative than simply building a big statue (a popular Australian method of kitsch tourism – see Big Pineapple, Big Merino, Big Prawn, to name a few), the course required input and investment from a raft of stakeholders to realise its ambitious vision. Eleven holes were purposely built within swinging distance of local roadhouses or visitor centres, with the remaining 7 holes being borrowed from existing local golf clubs. All combined, the Nullarbor Links measures a staggering 1365 kilometres from start to finish.

We have secured a campervan for the journey out of Adelaide and aim to knock off the 750 kilometres to Ceduna in an afternoon. Pushing north to the seaport town of Port Augusta, we stop for a photo at the Port Augusta Golf Course. This is our only taste of the Masters at the real Augusta, which plays out in the ensuing days as we devour road miles in the Australian outback with no phone or internet coverage.

Rounding the Spencer Gulf, the road veers to the west and the sun starts to dip lower and lower like a cracked egg yolk threatening a hot sizzling pan. The fading daylight hours align with a changing landscape, from bustling portside industry to the native and naked landscape of the Australian wilderness. Dusk feels like a changing of the guard: the roads clear of traffic, the nocturnal creatures begin the evening forage and the bush darkens to a deep red. A final push through the dark enables us to arrive by morning to catch the opening event of the annual Chasing The Sun (CTS) Tournament. It's a week-long travelling hoedown, drawing golf enthusiasts together to play the Nullarbor Links and share in local experiences both on and off the beaten track. The inaugural event was held to celebrate the opening of the course nine years ago, and remains popular amongst the mobile grey-nomad crowd.

A 9-hole Ambrose tournament at the Ceduna Golf Club provides a relaxing opening chapter – a chance to meet fellow participants, measure banter levels and acclimatise to the local golfing and weather conditions. We're not sure if the club members are pulling our leg when they instruct us to 'play the front 9' and to avoid the back 9 as 'it's a little dry'. It hasn't rained in six months, and with the dustbowl fairway of the 1st hole forcing us to dig our balls out of the raw earth, speculation is rife at just how dry the back 9 must be. What we are soon to learn, however, is that we're not in Kansas anymore: this is outback Australia, and they don't let something as meagre as a drought get in the way of a good time. As the beads of sweat gather and the bugs start to hover over my fresh scent, I schlepp up to the sandscape green of the 1st hole already covered in soil. This course sure has fight in it.

After a post-round pep talk from CTS tour leader Alf about the journey ahead (centred mainly on avoiding snakes), the afternoon's scheduled activity is a tour of a nearby oyster farm at eerily named Denial Bay. Following a hot tip, we stop in at the Ceduna Oyster Barn and indulge in a cheeky dozen of the freshest oysters you can imagine, complete with a Japanese-inspired dressing and lathered in vinegar, cucumber, ginger, wasabi and caviar. Perched on the rooftop of the café, with ocean views on one side and salt flats spanning into the desert on the other, we wonder if it's too early to call meal of the trip.

The following day we wake at sparrow's fart (really early in outback-speak) and are back at the Ceduna golf course for a champagne breakfast and a toast to the rising sun. A buzzy introduction to the week's entertainment from Bernie (a guitarist who provides music at all stops) and the playing of the first 2 holes marks the commencement of the event, and also the start of the Nullarbor Links course. It's a nice way to get a feel for the rhythm of outback golf, and speaks to the heart of the motivations of the course in drawing players into the local community.

After earning our rubber stamps we clamber into the van and embark on one of the world's most unique golfing adventures. It's a forty-five minute drive to the next settlement of Penong: just long enough to reflect on the starting holes, blast a full album of rock music to drown out the constant rattling of the van, and enjoy the meandering scenery of the Australian outback.

The par-4 at Windmills is a great little hole tucked away behind the local service station and married up to a flat of – you guessed it – windmills, which had previously been a vital part of water supply to the township in the past. Another reminder of Australia's reputation as the driest occupied continent. We refuel and continue west on to Wombat Hole at Nundroo.

The early afternoon sun beats down on Nundroo and as the temperature climbs into the low thirties, we question how feasible the course would be to complete in the blazing summer months. It is mid-autumn, yet our concentration levels are starting to be challenged by not only the weather, but another little pesky natural wonder: flies. Persistent, prolific and parched (they seem drawn to the moist parts of your body – think eyes, mouth and neck), club selection becomes not just a vital part of golf strategy, but a handy weapon of mass swiping. Not wanting to come across as the whingy young upstarts from the city, we keep our mouths shut (both literally and figuratively) until one of the hardened regulars mentions it in passing: in fact, it's the Lord Mayor of Kalgoorlie, John Bowler. John seems to be the most versed scholar in fly repellent remedies. His personal recommendation is a natural ointment used predominantly for the comfort of equine animals in and around his home town. His testimonial that 'if it'll keep the flies off a horse's arse, it'll keep 'em off your face' is as much of a stamp of approval as we need to priority-purchase a tub of said magical cream.

Hole 4 at Nundroo brings the first real test of our mettle and determination to actually complete this thing. A par-5, it presents a blind tee shot into the desert and no practical advice on where the ball should be hit. The fairway is a mix of broken rocks, small shrubbery and grey dirt – it immediately renders our decision to not bring any coloured balls a vital strategic mistake. We lose four balls between us getting to the green, and by the time we factor walking to the tee (most holes are one-way by nature), lost balls and holing out, it takes us nearly forty-five minutes to finish. We brush all the flies off our backs, reload the van and make a beeline to Coorabie, where we urgently mix a couple of strong G&Ts.

We are hosted by Debbie and Poggie, two fourth-generation sheep farmers who have opened up their property in the last ten years to host caravan and campervan travellers in the area. The CTS visit is one of the biggest nights of the social calendar for locals, with some Country Women's Association–inspired afternoon tea followed by the early opening of the farm bar (i.e. Poggie's son slinging crisp lagers from the fridge). There is enough lubrication to build excitement for the hole-in-one competition, which has golfers and locals thwacking a ball from the sheep-shearing shed across a paddock-cum-airstrip, pressing to claim nearest to the pin.

The evening spread of locally caught whiting with all the trimmings is washed down wonderfully with more cold lagers. Bernie provides the soundtrack for the night with a heartfelt solo offering, a band set of the classics, and a serendipitous duet between himself and Graham Hutchinson – a CTS participant who you may or may not know as the second prize winner in the recent Royal Caribbean Cruise Fiji karaoke competition. A bush dance ensues.

We make the mistake of trying to keep up with the locals and are thoroughly drunk under the table by some seasoned professionals, none more so than Marg Donkin, who together with her husband Eric, form the inspiring maintenance crew for the Nullarbor Links. They live in outback Western Australia and drive the course round trip every two months to ensure the greens are running well, the fairways are free of litter and nobody has stolen any flags. It's an extraordinary effort for the couple to have carried out these duties on a volunteer basis for nearly ten years.

Our idea of waking in the dark to catch the sun rising over the southern cliffs of the Australian coast seemed ambitious last night, and downright stupid now as our alarm rings at 5 am. We creep out of the farm in the van with a nod and silent farewell to our Chasing The Sun brethren. They sure knew how to have a good time.

The cliffs turn out to be much farther than we expect, or were told yesterday ('yeah, they're just up the road'), and we have to settle for sunrise at the very start of the Nullarbor Plain. We had shopped around the question of when (or where) the Nullarbor officially starts, with the typically Aussie response 'you'll fucken know, mate' becoming our new catchcry for the day. The term 'Nullarbor' was coined by surveyor EA Delisser, who combined the Latin terms 'nullus' and 'arbor', translating to 'no trees'. Even the indigenous term for the area, 'Oondiri', meaning 'waterless', seems to radiate a remarkably frank description of what the original inhabitants of the area saw in front of them. As we drive through the morning light, suddenly and without warning, the horizon empties out to a vast plain of red dirt and short pale green shrubs. There is not a tree for as far as the eye can see and in that moment … we fucken know.

Back to the golf.

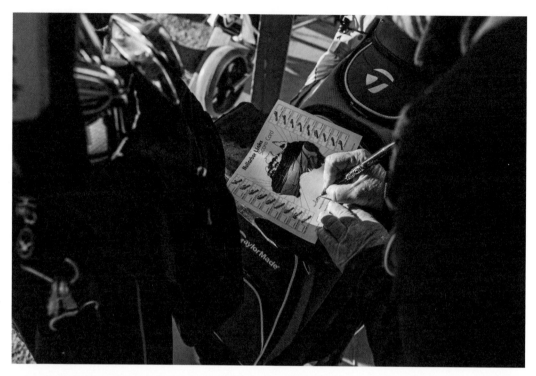

↑
Many of the greens are built from artificial turf, the best way to maintain a playable course in these extreme conditions.

↗
Us on the world's longest course.

→
Fly protection is highly recommended. You haven't seen flies until you've done the Nullarbor.

CONQUERING THE WORLD'S LONGEST GOLF COURSE

We arrive at the Nullarbor Roadhouse early to face another long and tricky par-5, along with a well-armed battalion of local flies. Perhaps it's our post-inebriated state catching up with us, but the mood of the hole is sombre. The trek in the dust past an abandoned airstrip seems to go on forever and both of us lose our first balls off the tee. Outback mythology dictates that a local crow takes the first ball of the day on this particular hole. This doesn't account for my following two balls though, and prompts a cursory glance at the scorecard to check how many more par-5s (i.e. lost balls) there will be. We're already running low both on esteem and balls so the idea of spending the next couple of days sifting through sandy scrub with a horde of flies for company seems tedious at best.

The drive from the Roadhouse ('Dingo's Den') to Border Village ('Border Kangaroo') is the longest span between holes at 184 kilometres (the shortest is 12 kilometres between Border and Eucla). On paper it looks like a drag, but as we take off we start to catch some wonderful glimpses of the limestone rock faces that make up this portion of the Great Australian Bight. There are a number of marked lookouts that provide jaw-dropping vistas of the 60 metre tall cliffs. Some preliminary research on our end had

also showed some unmarked roads (which we find) that give us uninterrupted access to spectacular Indian Ocean views. We park the van on the side of the cliff, pull out the annex, cook lunch and let the cool coastal breeze wash away the troubles of the morning.

We stop a few more times for photos and four hours later make it to the 6th hole. With an imposing kangaroo statue holding a tub of Vegemite overlooking the tee box, the par-3 feels like a clean slate. The sight of the flag only 160 metres in front of us is an absolute luxury and we close out the hole in record time, celebrate with iced coffees and bid a fond farewell to the state of South Australia.

We cross over the border to Western Australia, sacrifice some onboard fruit for quarantine purposes and enter a new micro-time-zone we have never heard of – Australian Central Western Standard Time – which runs at 8.45 hours ahead of UTC. In ten minutes we are chugging along a dusty path to the Eucla Golf Course, which plays host to the next hole. Again running short on daylight hours, we enjoy the inventive and practical nature of the course. The highlight holes of the Nullarbor Links seem to be ones where visitors can share spaces that provide a glimpse into the charged spirit of the local communities. The course is worn but brimming with character.

Onward through the Watering Hole, we arrive at Brumby's Run (Hole 9) well past dusk. After a brief run-in with a weathered truckie over the parking of our van, we decide to utilise some glow-in-the-dark balls and play the hole under the clear starry night. We press on to Cocklebiddy where a gravy-drowned schnitzel, some cold beers and a 9.5/10 hot shower round out a remarkable day.

The roadhouses along the way are really the lifeblood of the journey, providing weary travellers with stops to recuperate from driving and stock up on essentials. Most of the roadhouses aren't necessarily destinations in their own right and act merely as a servicing point along the route. Having said that, there is quite a bit of difference between the look and vibe of some of the offerings, and golfers are better off researching and planning their overnight stays.

Another dawn wake-up call as we tee off on Eagles Nest, only a few metres from where we have just slept. The naming of the hole becomes evident as we continue on to Caiguna – we see a number of majestic wedge-tailed eagles feasting on roadkill between shrubs on the side of the road. With a wingspan of 2.3 metres, they're easy to spot swooping through the barren landscape. We play the 11th hole before taking eating cues from the eagles and devouring some breakfast. The next part of the journey is tackling the 90 Mile

Straight, which registers as the second longest stretch of straight road in the whole world. Occasional dips in the road provide a remarkable sense of scale and we are left in awe of the Australian landscape.

Onto Skylab, which is probably this scribe's favourite hole of the course – no doubt due to a narrow miss on birdieing the hole from a dusty red chip shot. Another highlight of the Links is the little snippets of history included at each of the tee boxes. This par-3 at Balladonia takes its name from the NASA space station that orbited the earth between 1973 and 1979. Upon re-entry to the atmosphere, staff changed the direction of the station to land in the Indian Ocean south of Cape Town, with the hope of minimising impact on populated areas. Miscalculations and the unpredictable nature of the event meant that debris from the craft fell into the Indian Ocean and onto land in the Western Australian goldfields. Amid huge media interest worldwide, the local council and parks services team welcomed the Skylab investigation crew with a AUD400 fine (in jest) for littering as they arrived to inspect the missing parts.

We chug on through Sheep's Back and to the central town of Norseman, which plays host to two holes in Golden Horse and Ngadju. As we move further away from the Nullarbor Plain the landscape changes again, with an abundance of eucalyptus trees providing us company on the fringes of the road. The area is renowned for mining and the busy road industry provides a stark contrast to the sleepy nature of the Nullarbor.

The final travel stop is for Hole 16 (Silver Lake), part of the Kambalda Golf Club. The track barely has a blade of grass on it, with the brown-dirt greens making a low-maintenance course feasible in such an arid area. It's late in the day and with the clubhouse closed, we stamp our own scorecard from the chained-up stamp and hit the highway for the final stretch.

We arrive at our final destination to rapturous applause (from our own egos). After four days, three time zones, two states, 18 holes, twenty-three balls, 1365 kilometres and 20,421 flies we have made it to the end. The long straight road has taken us all the way to Kalgoorlie, which now feels like an oasis in the middle of the desert; a pot of gold at the end of the rainbow; the cherry on top of the proverbial cake. No discredit to Ceduna, but it's hard to imagine the same levels of elation had the course been played in reverse. Perhaps it's a result of the trials and tribulations of the previous days, but the well-manicured course at Kalgoorlie, resplendent with native flora and mobs of kangaroos, provides such a welcoming sight late in the day. We've climbed the mountain and the reward is the course. We savour some reflective time at sunset and decide to come back the following day to play the full 18.

With the luxury of time on our side, we enjoy a morning spent piecing together more than one play at a time – and not having to load and reload the van after each hole. The rich red dirt of the rough provides nice contrast and easy sighting for any stray shots. If the Nullarbor Links was camping then now we are sauntering around a five-star resort. We finish on a high and there is only one thing left to do: with a quick text message to the mayor, we are made privy to the location of his local repellent dealer. A quick stop in at Kalgoorlie Feed Barn to stock up on Nature's Botanical and we are now beyond prepared to take on any outback adventure again. With or without the flies.

Caddie Tips:

· It costs AUD70 to play the course; the fee includes a scorecard, map and brochures for local activities. Be sure to arrive stocked with an abundant supply of coloured balls. Unless you are Crocodile Hunter Woods, you will spend a lot of time searching through the scrub. Roadhouses sell some balls, but they are mostly souvenir editions which, for AUD6 or AUD7 a pop, can prove to be quite costly.

· Tee boxes are made from a concrete base and can be difficult to penetrate with traditional tees. You can fashion a Nullarbor tee by cutting off the top of a plastic water bottle and using the reverse side of the neck to cup the ball. Locals stipulate that the plastic bottle lid can also be used to prop up the ball on fairway shots.

· The synthetic greens are in great shape and are generally quite flat, allowing those with a banging short game to score well.

· The sandscrape greens require a bit of technique to get flat and generally roll pretty slow. A local tip is to apply firm pressure to the smoothing rake before the hole then ease off immediately afterwards, thus creating a stop ramp of sorts for overhit putts.

· The Links can be played west to east or vice versa, and is bookended by two holes at the Kalgoorlie and Ceduna golf courses respectively.

→

Leaderboards at Ceduna Golf Club.

→

(Next page) Looking out over the aptly named Great Australian Bight.

CEDUNA GOLF ASSOCIATES

CHAMPIONSHIP

DATE	B. GRADE.	C. GRADE.
1975	E.M. NEAVE.	J. VILLIERS.
1976	N. COOTE.	M. DAWES.
1977	S. WRIGHT.	J. HAMPEL.
1978	T. THISELTON.	R. HUNT.
1979	R. HUNT. ★	P. SARD.
1980	P. SARD.	N. COOTE.
1981	D. COLLINS.	C. CHALMERS.
1982	S. WRIGHT.	G. NISBET.
1983	P. GRIGG.	L. HURRELL.
1984	G. NISBET.	B. RYAN.
1985	S. WRIGHT.	D. LILLEY.
1986	S. WRIGHT.	N. SLEEP
1987	G. TREMAINE	J. MONTGOMERIE
1988	S. WRIGHT	J. GOODE ★
1989	T. THISELTON	G. RICHARDSON
1990	P. TAINSH	J. GOODE
1991	B. WEARNE	L. TREWARTHA
1992	B. WEARNE ★	D. COLMAN
1993	J. GOODE	N. TANGATAPOTO
1994	S. WRIGHT	V. SHIPARD
1995	P. SALE	L. HURRELL
1996	P. SALE	L. HURRELL
1997	P. SALE	L. HURRELL

HOLE IN

DATE	NAME	HOLE
8·6·58	BETTS. J. F.	9
2·9·62	PUCKRIDGE V.A.	13
15·5·68	BROWN. N.R.	13
11·5·69	KUTCHA. M.	13
6·8·72	KELLY. B.A.	9
30·12·80	COMAS. A.T.	17
3·6·81	MILLER. M.	14
13·6·82	MUIRSON. M.F.	6
8·9·82	THISELTON. T.C.	14
10·8·91	PARTINGTON A.	4
17·7·92	PRETTY H.	14
1·7·93	C. WEARNE	6
5.11.99	I. MacGOWAN	4
5.11.99	L. McWATERS	4
6.10.02	P. DAVIES	4
	K. McCARTHY	14

Land of the Silky Pear: Kalgoorlie

Words & Photography by William Watt

→

Layers of sand and turf at Kalgoorlie Golf Course.

The name Kalgoorlie is derived from the Aboriginal word 'karlkurla' which means 'silky pear', a native plant found in and around the Eastern Goldfields. Examples of the plant can be found around parts of this scenic course, one of the most distinctive in Australia. With its deep red soil and pristine fairways framed by a wide range of native plants, even the local kangaroos know they're onto a good thing here. Having just come from the dusty, barren lands of the Nullarbor Links, this felt like a golfing oasis in the desert.

Kalgoorlie itself exists primarily for the rich veins of gold that were found here in the late 1890s. Paddy Hannan, an Irish prospector, is said to have been the first to discover gold in the area, and found so much that it set off a major gold rush. Rumour has it that on the night of 14 June 1893, Hannan found gold in a gully in nearby Coolgardie. In an effort to keep the find low-key he concealed the gold and, during the night, along with two other Irishmen, moved one of his horses into the scrub. The next morning Hannan and company pretended to look for the horse in the scrub while the rest of prospecting party were about to head off – 'We'll catch up to you, lads!' After the main group had left, the three men returned to the gully and went about picking up the gold and pegging out their lease. Today mining is still a big part of the economy with the Super Pit gold mine, once Australia's largest open cut gold mine, still employing 1100 locals and processing 15 million tonnes of rock per year. Since gold was discovered in this area more than 58 million ounces have been found.

But even if gold isn't on your mind, you'll find some great nuggets on this well-routed Graham Marsh design. Marsh, a successful professional golfer and prolific course designer, was born in Kalgoorlie and might have given a bit of extra love in designing this course.

↑

The red sands and pristine fairways create some pleasing contrasts.

→

The shapely tee boxes are a feature of the Graham Marsh design.

Golf in a War Zone

Andrew Quilty takes a stroll with the locals through the golfing scene at Kabul Golf Club.

Words & Photography by Andrew Quilty

←

Golfers watch on from the 9th hole tee.

↙

Jawad (centre), one of Afghanistan's top golfers who says he has a handicap of 8, with Mohammad Afzal Abdul (right), the Kabul Golf Club's long-time pro.

When Mohammad Afzal Abdul returned to Afghanistan after the fall of the Taliban, he went straight to the golf course he'd first swung a club on at the age of eight. Located in a shallow valley of grey grass on the edge of Kabul, the golf course – from which Afzal, now fifty-five, had fled ten years earlier to seek refuge in neighbouring Pakistan – was barely recognisable.

'The grass was up to here,' Afzal says, pointing to his thigh, and the trees that once lined the fairways had been felled for firewood by those who'd remained behind during the civil war of the early 1990s and the Taliban rule that followed.

The biggest problem, however, was the likelihood that the course was now littered with unexploded ordnance and landmines. 'There were many rockets falling in this area,' he recalls of the time before he fled.

Impatient to bring Afghanistan's only golf course back to life, Afzal found an unusual way to dispose of the mines: he opened the gates and the sumptuous, grassy fairways to local shepherds and their flocks of sheep. 'They didn't know what was going on,' he laughs, inside the Kabul Golf Club's single-room clubhouse on a gloomy afternoon. Seeing a sheep or two blown apart by an anti-personnel mine would be preferable to a dead golfer, he thought.

The following decade of international military intervention saw the Afghan capital awash with foreign aid workers, diplomats, security contractors and American dollars. Even though it was far from the centre of the city where most foreigners were cloistered, for ten years the novelty of playing golf in Afghanistan drew a steady stream of enthusiasts to Kabul Golf Club (KGC) after its official opening in 2004. Some would return home from holidays with clubs salvaged from storage units and donate them to Afzal and a small but passionate group of golfers from the surrounding villages. With the mismatched clubs that accumulated, keen young locals Hamidullah, Jawad and Ali managed to whittle their handicaps down to single figures.

The twenty-somethings play the 9-hole, par-36 course religiously – while much of the rest of Kabul prays – on Friday mornings. Their attire is as eclectic as their selection of clubs: Jawad wears a Titleist cap, a TaylorMade polo shirt and golf spikes; Hamidullah, track pants and street shoes. They play throughout the warmer months with a handful of others whose scrappy swings belie entirely respectable scores.

Proper putting surfaces have never been within financial reach of Afzal's low-budget operation, and for many years, with typical Afghan ingenuity, Afzal jerry-rigged the greens using the few resources available – a compacted mixture of engine oil and sand.

←

Jawad and Ali celebrate after winning a play-off hole following a tied game of best ball.

↓

Zafar Khan, a caddie at the Kabul Golf Club, carries clubs for a more senior player on a cold, grey afternoon.

Despite the club's donated ride-on lawn mower, the fairways were always so patchy that repositioning one's lie to the nearest clump of grass has always been tolerated. As Hamidullah puts it, from what he's seen on television, 'an American course is like walking on carpet; here it's like walking on splinters'.

In 2014, the vast majority of foreign soldiers in Afghanistan withdrew from combat operations. Although international leaders declared that Afghanistan was ready to stand on its own two feet, since then the country has struggled with a faltering economy and a resurgent Taliban. Not to mention the rise of ISIS, which has claimed several devastating attacks, including a suicide bombing that took at least eighty lives at a peaceful protest in Kabul.

The KGC, like the rest of the country, has suffered. Afzal claims he hasn't had a foreigner play 'since [President] Karzai's time' – before 2014. He can no longer afford his oil-and-sand green treatment and so the putting surfaces are barely discernible from the fairways. On the green, players tamp down their paths to the hole with their putters.

The most committed players, like Hamidullah, can't afford the green fees. Resigned to the new reality, Afzal allows them to play for free. He says around a hundred people play for free each week, while sometimes 'rich Afghans' pay 1000 Afghani – a far cry from the USD50 fee foreigners used to pay.

By midday on Fridays the course is crowded. To Afzal and his acolytes' dismay, however, it isn't golfers populating the fairways. Young families picnic; groups of young men play cricket and soccer while local warlords stroll along the road that runs like a spine through the centre of the KGC, enjoying the relative security of the fenced-off course with their Kalashnikov-toting bodyguards in tow. The golfers have little choice but to call it a day after 9 holes.

With their golf clubs locked up inside the clubhouse, another KGC regular, Noor Ahmad, offers to walk with me to a hilltop high to the west, where an abandoned tank – a relic of the Soviet war of the 1980s – looms over the course. The barrel of its cannon points toward the 3rd tee in the valley below.

Once we've negotiated our way back down the mountainside, walking back along the road between fairways, Ahmad remonstrates with a young girl carrying a large rock that was protecting a sprinkler valve. She plans to use it as a wicket for her family's cricket match. A minute later, Ahmad's banging on a car window as the driver chews up the fairway trying to park his car. 'They don't even realise this is a golf course.'

←

Afzal shows a ride-on lawnmower that had been donated to the club. The club relies almost entirely on donations and the patronage of wealthy Afghans now. Most of the club's keen players, however, can't afford to pay, so Afzal allows them to play free of charge.

↗

Noor Ahmad, a keen golfer who speaks English but, for work, only drives a taxi because he's unable to find alternative employment, plays at the Kabul Golf Club regularly. Ahmad is pictured here in the doorway of the clubhouse.

Golf on the Edge of the World

NORTH ISLAND · NEW ZEALAND

For Renaissance man Tom Doak, creating golf courses is like penning timeless music albums. On location in Cape Kidnappers, William Watt riffs on artistry and imagination with one of the world's greatest course designers (and hits a few rounds in the process).

Words & Photography by William Watt

← *Fescue on the edge. The drop beyond is around 300 feet to the ocean.*

Cape Kidnappers holds mythical status in the golfing world. The unique images of cliff-edge fairways seem almost impossible. It's like a golf course you might see in your dreams, or imagine laid out on some unusual-looking piece of land while gazing out of your aeroplane window.

Which, it turns out, is exactly what American billionaire Julian Robertson did when he first flew over this remote cape on the east coast of New Zealand's North Island. However, unlike most, it was a challenge he was willing (and able – thanks in part to a stellar run on the US stock market) to take on, even after his preferred architect, Tom Doak, showed some reluctance to be involved. 'Julian might tell you I played hard to get on this one,' says Doak, one of the most sought after golf course architects in the world after a string of successful projects early in his career. 'I knew if we could build another great course on the heels of Pacific Dunes, then it would be much harder for people to dismiss that success as just having a great site. So, Cape Kidnappers [and Barnbougle Dunes] were crucial in putting my name up there as one of the best in the business for working with great sites, and that's been a great niche for me.'

It's a fair understatement – it must drive competing architects a little crazy to see some of the sites Doak has been approached with over the years, but he takes each site on its own merit and brings a strong degree of practicality to determine a site's feasibility. 'When I arrived in Napier, they picked me up in a helicopter and flew me across to meet Julian, so the first time I saw the site was as you see it pictured in the magazines, from the air rather than on the ground. We spent all day on the ground, and then at the end of the day, we went back to Napier via old two-track road, for miles and miles with a bunch of stream crossings. All I could think was, this entrance road is going to cost more to build than the golf course!' At a cool NZD11 million, it is certainly an extravagant driveway, and a testament to the determination required to build on such a remote site.

These days, a golf cart is all you need to get around at Cape Kidnappers, however, the routing across this difficult terrain is remarkable and walking the course is a must, something Doak was keen to ensure was possible from the outset. 'When I'm doing a routing, I am always thinking about how holes will fit together and what earthwork will be necessary. Most of the 5000 acres is quite rugged, so routing the golf course was a matter of finding the most gentle part of the property. On some of the more famous holes like 6 and 12 and 15, the contours didn't have to be changed much at all; in fact I played golf across the fields with my crew just as we were starting out, which was one of the most memorable rounds I've ever played. It had been a dry summer and the fields were grazed down tight by all the sheep and cows, so our drives had just as much rollout as they do today, maybe more. On the 6th I hit a sheep standing quite close to the stake we had placed to mark out the green, from across the ravine 200 yards away – the poor animal could not figure out what had happened! In the end we had to pass up some spectacular holes because building a bridge across at certain points was just not practical, or there was too much elevation change to take up. It was imperative to keep the course walkable, and once the bridges were built, it's actually pretty gentle to walk.'

While nailing down these technical elements is a crucial part of an architect's role, being able to harness the natural beauty of a site requires an artistic touch, particularly when dealing with a location as iconic as Cape Kidnappers. Doak explains: 'When you're near the ocean on hole 12 or 15, you look down at Hawkes Bay and you can see the waves coming in from miles out, like ripples on a pond after you throw a rock in. It took a lot of restraint not to build features that messed with the long horizon lines of the site … the first couple of bunkers we built looked like pimples on the landscape. We had to adapt, and limit our features to places where they hung down into the valleys, or off the edge of the world. But in doing so, we managed to keep the focus on the natural wonders of the site.'

This artistic side of the profession is where the most noticeable impression on the casual golfer is made, and it's where Doak really separates himself from many of his contemporaries. 'I've played golf with a couple of well-known musicians, and they say the process of writing a song is pretty similar to what I go through. Sometimes they'll wake up with a long string of lyrics or music in their heads, and sometimes they'll have to piece it together over a long period, even borrowing a piece they'd been working on years ago for a different song. I've done the same thing in finding golf holes to fit the ground.'

Playing the course, the first tee takes us inland with a relatively sedate tee shot and then requires a brave approach over a valley and around some classic, intimidating Doak bunkering. Bravery is something that becomes increasingly important throughout the round, as you edge around the farm and get a taste of the water views on hole 5 and especially hole 6 – a terrific par-3 over a valley with a generous landing zone and a green that encourages creativity. Truly enjoyable golf holes continue over valleys and ridges and build out towards the famous stretch of holes from 11 to 16, which, for a 5-hole stretch, would be hard to top anywhere in the world. If you can get out of here with the same ball you started with, you've had a bloody good run! Holes 14 and 15, two of the trademark ridge-running fairways, demand absolute accuracy but are still fun to play; even after hitting two balls in a row off a cliff on the Pirate's

Plank (hole 15) the experience doesn't suffer. In fact it's impossible to get grumpy at Cape Kidnappers – the course is too much fun, and a quick glance at the scenery in any direction will have lost balls soon forgotten. Most groups will linger on the 15th green and 16th tee for photographs and to soak up the stunning landscape – a nice touch here is that the generous course scheduling allows for such mid-round breaks. You can even take an hour (or two) for lunch after 9 holes if you desire, with the staff here genuinely wanting you to make a day of it.

Tee-shot selfies aside, the 16th is a cracking par-5, with a risk-reward drive followed by an enticing second shot to an elevated green – fall a little short though and there are deep bunkers waiting to punish those who really should have laid up. And punished you will be: the bunker sand throughout is coarse and difficult to get a feel for, which can make for costly flyers over clifftops (or so I've heard). The home stretch of two challenging par-4s means keeping your concentration up is important, even if you're no longer perched at the edge of land above Hawkes Bay.

Cape Kidnappers is a spectacular and distinct course from start to finish, and great fun as long as you're okay with a few calls of 'I didn't see that land, mate' as you watch your ball sail off into the ocean. The key here is to savour the challenge and soak up one of the most amazing landscapes in New Zealand.

Naming Cape Kidnappers

Captain James Cook is one of history's most prolific explorers, particularly around these southern shores. He also had a penchant for naming various discoveries during his travels and much of the New Zealand coastline still bears his occasionally whimsical names. During his voyage through here in 1769 he named the Bay of Islands, Bay of Plenty, Poverty Bay, Cape Farewell, Queen Charlotte Sound, Mount Egmont and Hawkes Bay. All either fairly literal interpretations of his impressions, or in honour of some British heritage. But Cape Kidnappers?

The story goes that when Cook was anchored off this cape on 15 October 1769 a Maori fishing boat sidled up to the *Endeavour* seeking trade. During the transaction, the Maori seized a Tahitian boy named Tiata, who was an on-board servant for Cook's interpreter. Why the Maori felt the need to abscond with Tiata is up for debate, but some suspect it was in retaliation for Cook's own kidnapping of three Maori in previous days, and that they perhaps believed the Tahitian was one of their own, still in custody. In any case, Cook's men opened fire on the Maori boat, killing two and injuring a third, giving Tiata the chance to leap back into the water and swim back to the *Endeavour* unhurt. The surviving Maori paddled back to shore, the attempted kidnapping (or rescue mission) a failure.

Cook wrote: 'This affair occasion'd my giveing this point of land the name of Cape Kidnappers.'

The Maori name for Cape Kidnappers is Mataupo Maui – the fish hook of Maui, the hero of Polynesian mythology.

The distinctive fingers of land make Cape Kidnappers one of the most remarkable golf courses on the planet.

The inland holes offer plenty of movement and strategic interest.

The Good, the Bad and the Bunkers

A sandy riff through the ins and outs of the bunker: St Andrews and beyond.

Words by Mark Horyna

'Good shot!' calls Fred, my American playing partner for the day. I smile wryly and wave over to the right side of the fairway, where he and his caddie are tiptoeing through the light rough, looking for his wayward second shot. Sighing, I head towards the small sliver of green set in front of the old stone wall. I'm pretty sure I've hit into the ruddy thing.

There are over 110 bunkers lurking on this course and up until now, I have quite luckily circumvented most of them. Okay, there is a short, but highly satisfying stint in Shell on the 11th hole, into which I send a nervously skulled chip shot skidding back over the sloping green. In the end, I manage to get out in one and hole my putt for bogey. Fred's caddie is laughing.

I miss Cheape's and the Principal's Nose, find my way around Sutherland, Cottage and the Students, just about carry the Pulpit and the Spectacles, happily ignore the Cat Trap, fly the Coffins, pass Boase's and the End hole. I'm lucky to miss Lion's Mouth. I carry the Beardies, pass Kitchen, Hell and the Graves, but find my way into Ginger Beer on the aptly named Long 14th. Swinging from Miss Granger's bosoms, I hit over Rob's and later just trickle past Wig on 16. But now, nearly at the very end of this wonderful round, my hooked 3-wood leads me towards disaster, finding its way into one of the golf world's most notorious card wreckers: the Road Bunker. Destroyer of dreams, defeater of wannabe champions. I'm on the feared 'Sands of Nakajima'.

Golf is a game of missed shots they say, and thus bunkers play a vital role. They come in all shapes and sizes. Some are long and shallow, many have clearly defined boundaries, while others seem to ooze into their surroundings, leaving the player in doubt of where they're standing. They are hazards perfectly carved into the land, filled with the whitest of sands to contrast the greenest of fairways. Some of the best, though, are ever-changing scars in the landscape, eroded by coastal winds and torrential rain. Others are deep, circular and pot-styled. Traditional bunkers, often found on links courses, come with grass-sod walls, their faces constructed out of strips of sod stacked nearly vertically from bottom to lip. Others are built with railroad ties. Here, a bad shot will ricochet like a bullet off the bunker face to a sometimes much worse lie.

DIGGING THE LINEAGE

While most modern-day water hazards, both frontal and lateral, are but a weak memento of the links land's original winding burns and windswept beaches, bunkers – even the most pristinely designed and manicured – bring us back to golf's true origins.

Golf began and evolved on ragged grounds along the Scottish coast. Agriculturally more or less useless dunescapes linking pastures and fields to the sea, these stretches of land were used for all sorts of purposes. Families would dry their linen on the windswept fields, archers would practise their skills, rabbits were bred or hunted, sheep would graze and early forms of shinty and golf were played. Burns, their dark water levels rising and sinking with the tidal movements of the sea, meandered between the dunes and brambles. Bare patches of sand on the tough but still damageable grassland were a common sight. These sandy spots were among the original forms of bunkers. Small animal scrapes that coastal winds would over time blow out of proportion gave early golfers bad lies and uneven stances. On the sides of steep dunes, sheep and rabbits would take shelter from gales and the frequently belting rain, their bodies leaving indentions in the ground. These hollows too would soon be torn open by the excavating wind.

Other bunkers formed due to natural dips in the land. Balls would funnel towards low points in the fairways, as golfers playing from there slashed the land. Soon, these growing patches of naked sand would become places to avoid. We can safely say that the earliest holes in golf evolved with and around these kinds of natural bunkers.

Later, greenkeepers would stabilise coincidental but interesting hazards. Among the first to formalise and actively manage bunkers was none other than Old Tom Morris of St Andrews. Modern course designers use bunkers not only as hazards but also as a means of visual stimulation and deception. Hazards are positioned to obstruct views, give depth to otherwise shallow or boring fairways, to force a certain line of play or encourage the stronger player to take risks. Good bunker placement can make a hole seem longer or shorter than it really is and can trick you into believing the green is closer or even larger. Strategically located bunkers can turn the blandest land into great golf holes. Laid out without inspiration or knowledge, they can ruin the best of courses.

There's also something to be said about how bunkers are viewed – and titled – as compared to water hazards. Water hazards generally stay anonymous. Although there are some fantastic ones, most aren't given specific names and certainly don't introduce themselves on scorecards and in course guides. Bunkers, on the other hand, have always attracted terrific titles.

Perhaps this is to do with the different kinds of penalty involved – hit into a water hazard, you pick up a one-stroke penalty, drop a new, shiny ball and get on with your game. No fight. But if you throw yourself into a bunker, the consequences might be a lot more severe. Many more dreams have been shattered in bunkers. Playing out of the sand, your fate lies in your own hands. Freeing yourself is up to your nerves and your own playing abilities. You can't simply drop a ball outside the hazard; you have to play as it lies and that, as we all know, can take a while. Bunkers mirror your skills, magnify your faults and can enlarge your incompetence. Consequently, it's no wonder that golfers find names for them: know your enemy! By naming your foe, you try to understand it; by understanding it, you might – but only might – conquer it.

NAMING NAMES

It would be an impossible task to attempt a ranking of the world's best bunkers. There are thousands worth mentioning. Many have names laden with history and legends: some of these echo terror and desperation and often a bunker's individual fame easily overshadows that of its eponym. Many (especially the newer ones) remain unnamed. Styles and designs differ; to compare Doak's rugged bunkers with Augusta's pristinely manicured hazards, for example, would be downright silly. As choosing the best is out of the question, here's a run-down of some of the most famous, the most feared, the most notorious.

Hell

The par-5 hole 14 on the Old Course in St Andrews is home to one of the most ferocious bunkers in the world. Just past the famous Elysian Fields, Hell is positioned on the very left of the fairway in a hollow, around 120 metres from the green, and is not only 2 metres deep, but expands for over 250 square metres. Hell has ruined many scores during its long and disastrous history. In the 1995 Open Championship, Jack Nicklaus needed four shots to extract himself from Hell, leading to an overall score of 10 for the hole. Though easy to find, Hell is difficult to leave. However, many will testify that its true terror lies in its surroundings. You'll find a few smaller pot bunkers en route to the green, awaiting any rescue shot left too short. These are aptly named the Graves, for reasons most obvious.

Coffin

On the west coast of Scotland lies Royal Troon, one of the world's best links, home to many Open Championships, windswept dunes, slippery greens, and – among ninety-seven other treacherous bunkers – the notorious Coffin. Standing on the 8th tee one might be tempted to underestimate the shot at hand. The Postage Stamp, a mere 110 metres long, is the shortest hole on the open rota, but with the prevailing wind coming in from the sea, the small green can be tough to find and even tougher to hold. To the left of the green, the narrow Coffin bunker (one of five protecting the hole) seems to suck shots in like a vacuum cleaner, and its steep sod-faced walls make escaping with the first shot not only a matter of skill but also one of good fortune. Labelled as one of the most fearsome holes in Scotland, Postage Stamp and the Coffin have destroyed the hopes of countless amateurs and pros alike. During the 1950 Open Championship, German amateur Hermann Tissies needed fifteen shots to finish the hole. Only one of them was a putt. At the 145th Championship in 2016, Bubba Watson carded a triple bogey after pulling his tee shot into the Coffin. After hitting his bunker shot over the green, he mis-hit his third and then two-putted for a six.

Himalayas

Once described by the *Telegraph* newspaper as a 'bunker you could lose a car in', the famous Himalayas at Royal St George's in Sandwich on the Kent coast of England is over 12 metres deep and 8 metres wide. Kept stable by wooden railroad sleepers on three sides, this classic bunker looms to the right of the 4th hole approximately 210 metres off the tee and beckons the long-hitter to try and carry it. Often copied by designers all around the world, the huge cavity nowadays only really comes into play when the wind is against you. Even if modern equipment can help, the simple sight of it will surely make even the best golfers slightly nervous. St George's member Ian Fleming immortalised the Himalayas in one of his James Bond novels – during a match against the archvillain Goldfinger, 007 manages to drive the bunker for a par-4. Today that score would be a birdie.

Church Pews

It seems impossible to write about bunkers without mentioning the terrifying Church Pews of Oakland. Measuring over 90 metres in length, and nearly 40 metres in width, this monstrous cathedral of sand, as it has been fittingly called, comes into play on the third and fourth fairway of the US Open venue and has put an early end to many hopeful rounds of golf.

Oakland was originally conceived by father and son HC and WC Fownes, both strict, some might say sadistic, advocates of the penal school of golf design. The original layout had over 350 bunkers and was meant to intimidate every golfer into submission. Prior to 1920, the Church Pews was not a single bunker, but a whole complex consisting of eight hazards. When the original bunkers were turned into one obscenely huge behemoth, the Church Pews were born. In 2005, designer Tom Fazio was asked to redesign it and keep it in play for the modern professionals. He added a number of yards to its length and four more grass banks to the existing eight. Successfully escaping the Church Pews is a difficult task. With hardly any room to swing between the turf islands, hitting the ball out sideways is the best of options for most golfers.

Cardinal

Another tremendous bunker complex that stretches the width of its fairway are the two hazards on Prestwick's par-5 3rd hole, Cardinal. Landing your first shot short of the bunkers on this tough hole will give you an intimidating panoramic view of the almost vertical bunker face lined with railroad ties. Your next shot needs to carry the full height of the wooden-clad hazard to find a narrow strip of bumpy fairway from where you can attack the green. American sportswriter Dan Jenkins, once dubbed 'the best' by Larry King, described the hole as one he'd like to 'gather up and mail to my top ten enemies'. Although Prestwick has long vanished from the Open rota, the club still hosts numerous amateur events, and Cardinal has lost nothing of its original excitement, danger and terror even to the best of players.

Hogan's Bunker

On a slightly lighter note, we need to mention a small bunker on one of Scotland's many hidden gems. At Panmure Golf Club, just a short drive from legendary Carnoustie (home of many brutal bunkers), Ben Hogan spent two weeks meticulously preparing for his first and only Open Championship appearance in 1953. Panmure's pleasant but testing links gave the 'wee ice mon', as the Scots soon came to call him, the perfect opportunity to hone the wide array of shots he needed to capture that year's Open Championship. His favourite hole at the small private club was the 6th, a slightly doglegged par-4 with a large but undulating driving zone and a slippery putting surface perched on top of a small dune. Hogan suggested building a little pot bunker to the front right of the green, thus making a precise approach an absolute necessity. Hit the ball slightly to the left and risk losing it in the long grass; miss to the right and find yourself in Hogan's, from where many shots have been blasted over the green to the dreaded deep hollow waiting behind it.

The Road Bunker

The Road Bunker is a legend. As an integral part of golf's greater consciousness, it is full of history and lore. Once dubbed 'golf's greatest heartbreaker', it is one of the game's toughest teachers. It has humbled the best. In 1978's Open Championship, Tommy Nakajima was one shot off the lead, when he unluckily putted his ball into the bunker after reaching the green in two. He subsequently needed four shots to find his way out again and finished the hole with a nine. The bunker has since then been nicknamed the Sands of Nakajima. In 1995, Costantino Rocca – who had on the 18th hole made one of the most astonishing putts of all time to force himself into a play-off with John 'Wild Thing' Daly – found himself in this bunker. Unable to play out, Rocca left his dream of picking up the Claret Jug in the sand.

The Road Bunker has been around for ages. Historians believe it dates back to the early beginnings of the Old Course. The people of St Andrews used to dig for shells on the links, and one of the preferred spots was where the Road Bunker now lies. Old as it is, it has constantly evolved. It has grown larger and wider, deeper and steeper over the centuries. Today's version is much more severe than the one Nakajima had to play out of. ⚑

The Longest Hole

ALL OVER
•   •
MONGOLIA

An epic single-hole golfing odyssey through some of the harshest terrain on the planet.

Words & Interview by Dave Carswell
Photography by Andrew King

It was rugby that first brought Adam Rolston and Ron Rutland together when the two met in Hong Kong while playing professionally for a local team. It is golf, however, that will be the enduring legacy of the pair, as they recently completed a 2011 kilometre trek across Mongolia in an adventure that they (and the *Guinness Book of World Records*) have dubbed 'The World's Longest Hole'.

It was a half-baked idea that somehow came together, combining Rolston's love for the game and Rutland's experience with intrepid adventures. The latter once cycled from South Africa to England over the course of two years for the Rugby World Cup, only to see his beloved Springboks get beaten by Japan in one of the biggest upsets in the sport's history. There was no such heartache in Mongolia as the two set off from the westernmost base of Khüiten Peak, heading east with the view of reaching the 18th hole at Mt Bogd Golf Club (one of two golf courses in the country) by the time their ninety-day visitor visas had expired.

With Adam hitting an average of 250 shots a day, Ron, as the caddie, was tasked with managing their cart: traversing their housing, food, 30 kilograms of extra golf balls and other belongings along the varied landscape. A custom-made app tracked the shot count and route, officiating their record attempt. A few days into the trip they were joined by a wild Mongolian dog they named 'UB' (an abbreviation of the capital Ulaanbaatar) and the three of them set out with determination on their sleeves and the horizon in their sights.

The trio faced a raft of challenges, with the laborious terrain of the mountains and the unforgiving Gobi Desert, ever-changing weather conditions, and trying to maintain sobriety in the face of enthusiastic locals keen to get sauced on fermented horse milk and Russian-grade vodka. Despite earlier setbacks, the trio reached Mt Bogd on schedule, having hit 20,093 strokes over eighty days. In the process they managed to raise money for golf development in South Africa and for the Laureus charity, which uses sport as a powerful vehicle in breaking down discrimination and disadvantage.

Even though Rolston's initial estimates were for parring the hole at 14,000 strokes, we will forgive him for not mentioning his 6000 over. We sat down with the guys to discuss planning for the trip, the physical strain of playing golf all day, and carrying a putter for eighty days with a niggling fear that it may not get used.

The thought of hitting a golf ball around Mongolia sounds like something it was cooked up over a few beers at a pub. How did you come up with the idea?
RR: I think what will surprise you is it wasn't started over a beer. Adam and I actually know each other from rugby days in Hong Kong. I used to live out there, we'd go to the same club, and Adam was playing professionally for Hong Kong. Last year, Hong Kong were on tour playing two games for Kenya in Nairobi, and I was out there, and met the team, and shared some stories about a previous adventure I'd done. Over dinner and a cup of coffee Adam came up with the idea of doing a golfing adventure. I'd been to Mongolia before, and we put two and two together. Less than a year later we were putting out on the 18th hole at Mt Bogd Golf Club in Mongolia. It was crazy the idea started over a cup of coffee, but even crazier that we actually got to the start line.

How much organisation went into the trip in terms of logistics, and preparation, in the lead-up to going?
RR: It pretty much was all consuming, I'd say, for probably five or six months, from conception to tee off. I'd been there before and realised it was a country of no fences really, unlike anywhere in the world. If you wanted to do something like this [elsewhere], you would need permission from people and permits. One of the beauties of Mongolia is its absolute freedom. The difficulty was the logistics of how we're going to find a 2000 kilometre route that's going to be feasible to play golf along. You can refer to Google Maps and think it looks fantastic from the sky, but you get there and you come over a mountain pass and the grass is waist length.

We spent a lot of time plotting and planning the route ourselves, and we found a Mongolian expedition guide who knew the country very well. Together with him we plotted the route and the logistics around the dates, because there is only a very short window in Mongolia. Ulaanbaatar is the coldest capital city in the world, and it's pretty much a four-month window where we could actually squeeze our ninety-day or eighty-day expedition into, so we had a bit of time pressure from that point of view – and then it was getting on board, and one of the big things from a caddying point of view, was how in the world are we going to lug this stuff across the country? We wanted to be as authentic as possible and walk it. A lot of time went into designing the cart, and obviously going backwards and forwards, deciding exactly what we were going to take, because we're going from some of the coldest conditions to some of the hottest conditions. Then obviously getting sponsors and partners involved. Getting TaylorMade, who very generously sponsored us 400 golf balls and the clubs, finding a technology partner who built an app for us so that we could GPS-record every single shot, so when it comes to the world record, we've got a verification of what we actually did.

Did you do anything in terms of physical preparation before going out there, to make sure that you were fit enough?
AR: For me, I thought it was actually going to be tougher in terms of swinging a golf club. If you go to the range, you maybe hit 150 balls, and you probably hit them one every twenty seconds. I'm hitting a golf ball and then walking – it's like a golf shot on a golf course, you don't just constantly hit balls. You hit, you walk, you hit, you walk, and I probably did that 250 times a day. I think Ron's job was much more physical.

RR: I think what was most tiring was the fact that we had to do it for eighty days in a row. Any one particular day – some of them were tough – it was having to wake up the next morning. We had a ninety-day visa, but the eighty days was our target and we set ourselves a pretty aggressive schedule. I think in the whole of eighty days, we only had about three or four days off. But I also think Adam's being a little bit modest or playing it down a bit, but I think the challenge for him as well is he had to carry to help take a bit of the weight in the cart.

Was there a turning point, or did it just slowly get easier over time?
RR: Basically the way we chose the tee boxes, once we established that we had permission from the golf club to finish on their 18th green, we placed the tee box the furthest point you could possibly find in Mongolia from the 18th green, which meant it was at the base camp of the highest peak [Khüiten Peak] – which sits at the border between Kazakhstan, Russia, China and Mongolia. So it really was high up in the mountains, and completely ill-suited to what we were trying to do in terms of golf, but after that first four or five days when we eventually got down to the valley floor, I wouldn't say it was easy, but certainly easier.

Then, I think once we probably had two or three days in a row of our initial target of 25 kilometres, our bodies started getting used to the demands – the human body is incredible how it conditions itself to what it needs to do. I think once we had a couple of days under our belt, we actually got through those days relatively easily and we felt quite good, and thought perhaps we might just be able to catch this up and make time. So, I'd say it was probably the first time we did 25 kilometres in a day would have been a significant milestone.

Professional golfers can get quite temperamental with their caddies. Adam, you were stuck with Ron for eighty-two days. What were Ron's responsibilities outside of club selection?
AR: Well, a caddie on a normal golf course really doesn't have to carry the food and the accommodation for the duration of eighty

days, so the caddie pretty much only has to carry bananas and water and the clubs for four hours. Ron was tugging this 100 kilogram piece of kit 80 kilometres a day, every day. It included our whole life in behind him, so it was very different to a normal caddie.

RR: Less technical – brute force is probably the best description.

You started the journey as a twosome and were soon joined by a dog who finished the journey with you. How did you meet the dog?
AR: It's quite a cool story, considering no dog has probably walked that far [2000 kilometres] in Mongolia. He's actually the nomadic Mongolian breed of dog, so he became quite famous on social media. People were taking photographs of him and posting it up, and he had quite a bit of a following at the end of it.

I always had it in the back of my mind, 'This dog can never come home with me, he's too big, and too wild, and too old to come back to Hong Kong, or wherever,' so we started putting a plan in place two weeks before the end, trying to find him a good home. So holding the putt on 18, it felt slightly … it was an awesome feeling finishing off this massive adventure, but we had this partner in crime that didn't have a home and there was a lot up in the air. So we went into the national park, which is quite close to Ulaanbaatar. We couldn't get him into a car, because he'd never been in a car, so we rented a bus. We took him to this tourist Ger camp – there was a nice little plot of land down at the bottom of the valley, the most beautiful place in the world.

We explained to the guy that looks after the Ger camp how famous this dog is and how much we love him, and asked whether he would take the dog on. And he was completely over the moon that we had chosen him to take the dog. It just turned out so well, and in the morning it was very emotional leaving the dog behind. The guy had already started making a house for him, and it was just the most amazing end to our journey, but also for the documentary; it was just a really good full stop.

Obviously golf is not a massive sport in Mongolia, is it correct that the course that you finished at is the only golf course in the country?
RR: There's two proper golf courses, but this is sort of the flagship golf club of Mongolia. There's only two in the country that have grass greens, and there's one with artificial greens. All of these golf courses are less than ten years old. Mongolia slowly crept out of the end of Communism of the late 1980s, early 1990s, but it's only over the last fifteen years [that] the economy has developed. I guess golf is a game that people take up when there's money around, so that's the short history of golf as far as we understand it in Mongolia. Outside of the capital city, in the west where we started, people have absolutely no idea … I'd say there was about 20 per cent of people who recognised what the game of golf was.

How were you received when locals saw two white guys and a golf club, a little cart and a black Mongolian dog walking along? Was there a lot of interest in what you were doing?
AR: Yeah, we almost felt like the world's ambassadors for golf. In a way, we were like–

RR: Introducing this game to the world.

AR: I actually think that more attention was put on Ron and the cart: they were like 'why the hell are you walking?'

These guys would just be there with cigarettes, or a few beers, just having whacks and all having a good time. Honestly, the amount of times we saw guys shoulder-width apart, they've got the right hand over the left, and have just struck it 140 yards with an 8-iron, first up. They've just seen me hit a ball, and they just get it – it's so weird. I think it's gotta be something to do with being quite coordinated, because they ride horses, and they wrestle, and they fire bows off horses. I think Mongolians love golf, they just don't know it yet.

How did you go communicating with locals?
RR: We had a magic letter. Well, we called it a magic letter but it was just a letter. Before we left we translated a letter explaining who we were, where we're from, why we were out there, thanking people in advance for their kindness and hospitality, and explaining the journey and the fundraising aspect. The guy who helped us plan the route then translated it into Kazakh and Mongolian, the two main languages, and then we got a photograph of Adam and myself photoshopped with Mongolia's most famous sportsperson. He's this Mongolian wrestler who won some Japanese sumo contest and he's probably the Shane Warne of Mongolia. We would pull this letter out, all laminated, and people would read it. Again, the thing that they were most surprised about was why would somebody choose to walk. But despite being a world apart culturally and physically, people are good people and they just understood our mission, and understood we'd need food and water, and were generally very kind to us.

What was going through your mind coming to the end of your adventure?
AR: When the time came, I had a rusty 8-iron from 120 yards. I found the front edge of the green with 55 feet, pushed it past by 8 feet. I thought, 'Ron, we've been thinking about this moment for so long, and it's actually come and it's the worst scenario possible. I've just got this slippery putt down the hill.' And yeah, we ended up holing it, and it was just such an awesome way to finish.

For twelve weeks I thought I was going to 3-putt, you know? So that was a very satisfying moment. It was like an absolute full-stop ending to the whole trip. In front of 250 people with cameras and everything, Tiger fist-pumping and people going bananas. People said stuff like 'oh, it'll just be an extra shot on your 20,093 shots or 94 shots,' but honestly, it was one of the best moments of my life, without a shadow of a doubt.

RR: I had to lug this putter all the way, 2000 kilometres – and my biggest fear was that Adam was going to chip, and we'd never use it.

AR: We carried the driver, and the driver got hit twice, because we had to hit a provisional off the tee box just in case we lost the first one. And then the putter was only hit twice.

I guess now that the trip has been completed, has it inspired any other ideas about travel and exploration, or are you content with your achievements and looking to have a break?
AR: I would say for me, I'm not going to do an adventure very soon. I got everything I wanted out of it, I left everything out there, I wouldn't change anything, no regrets. But what I would say is, other challenges have become much easier in my head. It is such a phenomenal thing for people to do to just get out, and just break stereotype, and don't worry about what people say, and the dangers of things. Just get out there, and have a bloody good laugh, and just go hard.

King Island

BASS STRAIT · AUSTRALIA ·

Just forty minutes from Melbourne lies a whole other world. King Island might be small, but it's packed full of surprises.

Words & Photography by William Watt & Dave Carswell

←

Martha Lavinia is one of the best surf spots in Australia and just fifteen minutes from Cape Wickham.

Near the northern tip of King island, we get our first glimpse of the Cape Wickham lighthouse. Built in 1861 in response to yet another deadly shipwreck, it stands at 48 metres and is Australia's tallest lighthouse. Built from locally quarried stone, the thick, tapered walls have stood against some fierce storms and not moved an inch in its 158 years of warding off ships from the intrepid cape coastline – one that just so happens to be perfect for golf.

CAPE WICKHAM

'I just saw it and went "wow"', recalls Andrew Purchase, who first found the piece of land at Cape Wickham. 'I was over there looking around at various properties, getting a feel for what the land was like. We'd looked at lots of sites all over Australia. I bumped into the local real estate guy on the street, and he said that there was a piece of land on the very northern tip of the island, up near the Wickham lighthouse. So I jumped in the car, and headed up there with him for a look. It was 280 acres, I think, that were originally for sale. I fell in love with it.'

Purchase was no stranger to the golf business, having established a golf course construction and maintenance business in the early 2000s, and being involved in several high-profile projects both near his hometown of St Andrews Beach on Victoria's Mornington Peninsula and further afield. 'I knew we could do something pretty amazing with it, but obviously pending various permits and going through that whole process was an unknown. It was extremely sensitive with the shearwaters, the mutton birds. There was a whole colony there. But we took a risk and bit the bullet and I bought the land pretty much straight away.'

Risk comes in different levels. There's the 'asking someone out on a date' sort of risk. The risk of eating dubious street food in a foreign country. Then there's buying a huge chunk of land on a really remote island off the Tasmanian coast, with the intention to build a golf course on it, and no guarantee you're even allowed to do it.

Then there's nearly doubling down on that risk. 'I got Darius Oliver to come down and have a look at what we had,' says Purchase. 'His initial thoughts were that we needed to get closer to the water, and that it would be best to acquire another hundred acres, which was to the south of what we already had. I managed to buy that land. Darius got in touch with Mike DeVries. I flew Mike over, and said, "Off you go, just get the best you can out of it." Which they did. And it was pretty collaborative, actually, the routing between Mike and Darius.'

Purchase took the plans to Hobart and, as expected, the process for approval was far from straightforward. Eventually they got the go-ahead, but with a catch – they could only build while the local bird colony was out of town. Which is for three months. In the dead of winter.

'The golden rule when you're working in those sort of sites is you go hole by hole. You irrigate it so you can protect it from wind erosion and all those things. We didn't have that option. We had to have it all done, basically bogged in, when the birds migrated back to King Island. It wasn't ideal and it put a real lot of pressure on us – we're already sitting out in the middle of Bass Strait, and it was the wettest and windiest winter in eighty-eight years. It was Murphy's Law, you know?'

With the course bulked in across those three wet and windy months, it was down to shaping and grassing work for those six months of the schedule. Things didn't get any easier. Several holes washed away overnight, and many holes were grassed multiple times. Purchase recalls that the seaside par-3 11th was grassed five times before it finally had a chance to settle – 7 metre swells took the tees straight out to sea.

'I think the hardest thing was, from my point of view, keeping the morale of the team together. You're driving up there in the morning, it's pitch black, you come home at night, it's pitch black. And then you see your work just vaporise before you. The guys are sort of like "Really? Do we have to do this again?" But yeah, they were amazing. A really, really good team. You've got to look after yourselves. There's obviously some danger there as well, especially in the initial stages, as you've got quite a lot of snakes. You don't want to get hurt up there, because you're an hour away from help. So everyone sort of looked out for each other, and we made sure that we did things as safely as possible.'

The risk, and hard work, paid off – a course emerged that exceeded Purchase's highest expectations. And the plaudits came in thick and fast, with Wickham debuting remarkably high on various top 100 lists in its first year.

PLAYING WICKHAM

We'd heard all the buzz about Wickham in its first year, and seen all the photos. But in the back of my mind I wondered if somewhere so exposed, so raw, could really be all that was being claimed. It didn't take long for those qualms to be dispelled. The practice putting green melds seamlessly into the first teeing ground – it's immediately clear that this place has been built with an attention to detail and craft that belies its rugged setting. I glance down the first fairway with its roaring ocean whitecaps beyond. Then a look across to the impressive lighthouse, with a pristine cove in the foreground. That and a few amazing-looking golf holes draped across the land. But back to the task at hand – hitting that first fairway.

The first green complex impresses again – understated, but utterly unique and memorable. There's a seamless connection to the clifftop 2nd tee (definitely a walking course; leave the carts at the clubhouse). It leads us around the coastline to the par-3 3rd: a shot played over rocks and crashing waves to a generous but beautifully contoured green. Extraordinarily, 11 holes at Wickham either start, finish or run alongside the jagged coastline, and there are only a couple of holes that don't feature ocean views (they're also some of the best on the course). There are a few holes, like the par-4 4th, where local knowledge and a well-honed ground game offer a distinct advantage. Sloping front-to-back and playing downwind, trying to hold the green here without using the ground game is

←

The 18th fairway at Cape Wickham wraps around Victoria Cove.

→

Top down on the par-5 15th at Cape Wickham.

nigh-on impossible, and the wide extensive run-off area behind the hole that borders the first green suddenly makes a lot more sense. The short par-5 6th is the first hole to play inland and has a brilliant green complex that allows pin position to determine your strategy for the hole. Bunkered into the dunes and offering shelter from the relentless westerlies, it encourages players to drop a ball and have a roll at some potential alternative pin locations and take a breath after a blistering opening.

The 7th is a frustrating par-3 that plays across a diagonal valley and features a huge dune mound just short of the green, which otherwise would be the only sensible place to land a ball if the prevailing wind is up. Ejections all round. After the challenging 8th takes you up a beautiful sand dune–bordered valley, the epic par-5 9th launches you back towards the ocean and directly into the breeze. The topography here is off the charts. Navigated properly, birdies and even eagles are possible. Get out of position though and there are sizeable dunes and valleys that'll eat you up. The 10th plays sharply downhill to the ocean's edge – hit the fairway and the approach shot here is one you won't forget. As the salt spray lashes my face on the 11th tee, I'm reminded that it took several attempts to build such an ambitious hole. But I'm sure glad they persevered – this and the short par-4 12th are what Wickham, and King Island, is all about: wind, craggy rocks, crashing waves, wallabies, limestone cliffs. Daring golf. Turning with the wind behind us on hole 13 is a relief, and two good shots here give you a decent chance to score and part ways with the western side of the course on good terms. Wandering past the (still) temporary clubhouse to the 14th brings

us to those holes we spied over from the 1st tee, which are worthy of more than a fleeting glance.

With the ever-present Cape Wickham lighthouse taking a prominent position above the approach to the punchbowl 14th green and par-5 15th tee, we're conscious of enjoying the respite of downwind holes and prepare for the run home that we can see stretching along the coastline to our left. The 16th, a spectacular par-4 with a stepped fairway that feeds down towards the rocky ocean, includes a scenic boardwalk across the rocky shoreline, just in case you need more ocean vibes. By the time we make it to the 17th tee, it's all just getting a bit ridiculous (in a good way). A beautiful par-3 awaits, as well as a great view of what the 18th, with its very own beach bunker, has in store. Victoria Cove, a lovely little inlet with a pristine white sandy beach, stretches the length of the hole, and is in play should you bite off a little too much with the driver. As bunkers go, it's hard to think of anything this cool. At the northern tip of a tiny island in Bass Strait, with the waves literally lapping at your feet, you can attempt a heroic recovery back up onto the natural shelf above the beach. An exhilarating finish to a breathtaking round. A beer is now required.

Post-round, the marquee clubhouse brings welcome shelter from the winds, and is buzzing with golfers from around the world reviewing their experience. Nobody is disappointed with what they found here. Andrew Purchase fell in love with the land before there was even a stake in the ground. Then he and the design team were able to build a superb golf course on it. It's safe to say golfers will be falling in love with it for many years to come.

The 1st green at Cape Wickham is understated but unforgettable.

The walk down the 1st fairway at Cape Wickham. This is golf.

Riding the dunes.

↑

The rugged par-3 4th
at Ocean Dunes.

OCEAN DUNES

Just ten minutes north of the main town of Currie sits Ocean Dunes, a Graeme Grant–designed 18-hole layout that's as bold and challenging as it is scenic. While Cape Wickham is the headline act on King Island, Ocean Dunes is a worthy warm-up, and if you've made it this far, a must play. Grant, a former superintendent at Kingston Heath Golf Club, was the main driver behind the project, purchasing the land, designing the course and leading the building process.

The understated car park and pro shop on arrival mean we are under no illusions – this is a pure golf experience. Ocean Dunes has a routing that requires some significant treks between some holes and carts are strongly encouraged, but we're up for the walk despite already punching out 18 at Wickham earlier that morning. Dunes is a rollicking ride, and there are moments across the property that are quite breathtaking. The first of these is wandering up the first fairway, past the giant blowout fairway bunker, and into a vast landing zone bowl of pure fescue. It's quite disorientating, such is the scale – Grant has been careful throughout the course to provide wide landing zones, mindful of the prevailing winds endemic of this island.

The front 9 provides a contrast of sheltered green sites, some neatly surrounded by dunes, and others positioned spectacularly along the coastline. The standout is the par-3 4th, a 130 metre shot into the prevailing breeze across an inlet to a large, shapely green surrounded by gnarly natural rock formations and colourful succulent plants. It's spectacular, and anything on the dance floor feels like a win here. This again contrasts with some of the inland holes, which are designed to assist a wayward approach and use the greenside dunes to great effect. The 6th and 7th in particular offer fun approaches, where the option to aim away from the pin and watch the ball roll is definitely in play. The 9th delivers a great strategic par-5 – it plays relatively short downwind, and given the split fairway a driver may not be the best club here. Finding a good angle to take into the sharply angled green site is a more important

consideration – a pin on the top tier might call for a lay-up, whereas the lower portion of the green is all too tempting for most.

The back 9 is situated north of the clubhouse, and as we descend to the 10th tee we can't help but think that there might have been a way to utilise the hard-earned elevation to better effect. But the walk is worth it – the 10th is a long par-3 that plays across the Southern Ocean, with the wind helping keep you on dry land. Holes 12, 13 and 14 all work around a huge sand dune – a definitive feature of this back 9 – with the downhill 14th offering some of the best views of the property. At just 126 metres, it's only a wedge even into the breeze, but the bold contour means it's a hard green to hit, and there are no easy up-and-downs.

The blind tee shot at the par-4 15th eventually links up with the 12th at a gigantic, undulating double green site – allow a few minutes to roll some putts around here. The 16th, running towards the ocean with a Scottish-style burn up the right edge of the fairway, is a back 9 highlight, often requiring a long iron approach to one of the most nuanced greens on the course. A good approach here is likely to provide one of the highlights of the day. Holes 17 and 18 are both strong par-4s, requiring accurate lines off the tee for a fun finish for match play.

Visually, Ocean Dunes offers a greater array of layers and textures than even Cape Wickham, and throughout the routing you'll find yourself in some truly surprising settings and backdrops. Depending on your taste, several holes here would make it into a best 18 on the island. There's also a good connection with the local community here – they run a weekly competition for locals at discounted rates, and also collaborate with the King Island Hotel to accommodate golfers in the heart of Currie. Pack your best walking shoes if you're up for hoofing it, otherwise this is a place where taking a cart won't draw any judgement. Dunes was always destined to sit in the shadow of Cape Wickham given the iconic land that Wickham is built upon. But that's certainly no second prize – Dunes remains a worthy golf course and an integral part of the King Island golfing experience.

↑
The opening stretch of holes at Ocean Dunes hugs the coastline and mirrors the ocean.

↖
Above the par-3 4th.

←
King Island is a tough environment for trees.

Golf on the Outer Hebrides

SOUTH UIST

SCOTLAND

Global wanderer and weekend hacker Ben Renick traipses the mystical landscapes of the Isle of Skye in pursuit of Old Tom, mythic Askernish and the Outer Hebrides.

Words by Ben Renick
Photography by William Watt & Rosie Giles

T he Isle of Skye can be summed up in a word – remote. Known for its rugged landscapes, the Scottish isle's sprawling mix of lochs, peninsulas, mountain ranges and rock formations is as mystical as it is jaw-dropping.

My wife, Anne, and I have travelled to Scotland with Will Watt and his wife, Rosie, somewhat crashing their honeymoon. After five days at Glastonbury Music Festival, the four of us drove 1100 kilometres north to get here, the road trip via Edinburgh providing a much-needed sense of calm after a hectic festival experience. But as beautifully calming as Skye is, there's an ulterior motive to our pilgrimage: South Uist Island, a ferry-ride away and home to the Old Tom Morris–designed Askernish Golf Club. First, a few days to unwind on the misty isle.

THE EPIC ISLE

The drive over the bridge from the UK mainland takes longer than expected due to the amount of photo opportunities at every bend in the road – and there are many bends. As we take in the view over the paddocks, across the ranges and out to sea, the sun begins to set and we finally reach our resting place for the next three nights.

A few days on the Isle of Skye really gives you an insight into island life. The roads are largely one-way, with turnouts strategically positioned to allow passing and overtaking. The thank-you wave (of which there are many incarnations) quickly becomes a much-used custom, more so for me after some stern words of advice from a local bus driver after failing to use a turnout when I should have. Portree is the biggest town on the island and is surprisingly bustling with tourists, to the point where it's near impossible to get a table for dinner at one of the few pubs, let alone a car park. The coastal

drives are magnificent, past the sea of quaint white cottages which are scattered across the fields of grazing cattle and sheep. I didn't have time to research it, but it seems likely that anything other than a white single-storey cottage is against local planning regulations. Skye is a crofting community – a croft being a small holding of land, usually of only a few acres. There are more than 2000 crofts on the Isle of Skye but only a few are large enough for the crofter to earn a living solely from it, so most band together in a social system of working communities to make a living.

Given its epic landscapes, Skye is also the land of myths: like the Storr on the east coast, a collection of large zeniths of rock formed by landslides in ancient times. Legend has it that the giant Old Man of Storr was buried with his fingers sticking out, creating the peaks. Or the Fairy Pools, a natural waterfall phenomenon that highlights vivid blues and greens in the water, causing a supernatural feel akin to the woods of Twin Peaks. It is no wonder the makers of *Game of Thrones* chose Skye as one of the premier locations for filming.

OLD TOM AND MYTHIC ASKERNISH

It is rare to be graced with a clear day on the Outer Hebrides, and the day of our ferry trip proves a happy anomaly. There is a saying around these parts – beautiful one day, raining the next. And another: windy one day, very windy the next. (NB: sayings may have been coined by the author mid-trip.)

After the ferry across from Skye, the real sense of island life hits home as we drive past the wreckages of old farmhouses dotted along the road to Askernish. The population of South Uist – the second largest of the Outer Hebrides islands – is only 1700 (and in decline). We barely see a soul on the 40 kilometre drive to the course. From the Lochmaddy port we set off from North Uist across the bridge to the south. Sheep and goats own the roads here and prove a formidable obstacle. Lakes and rivers scatter the landscape with mountain ranges in the distance. We pass signs warning us to look out for otters crossing the roads, but alas don't catch sight of any.

Though its roots are mythic, the modern incarnation of Askernish began in 2005. Gordon Irvine, a golf course consultant, was looking for a new and exciting destination for a sporting holiday with friends, when he heard that there was a golf course on the island of South Uist designed by Old Tom Morris. Irvine found this hard to believe at first. Old Tom Morris is the father of golf and most famous for designing the home of golf, St Andrews Golf Course. How could there possibly be another course designed by him so far off the beaten track?

The story goes that Old Tom was lured to South Uist in 1891 by the sheer abundance of land available on which to design the perfect links. After surveying the west coast, he decided that Askernish farm would be the location for his project. In its early years the course was used to bring visitors to the island, and was successfully maintained until 1922 at which point it was claimed by local crofters for their day-to-day pursuits. Since then, the Askernish Golf Club has had a tumultuous history and has undergone many layout changes. It briefly shared its land with an airport, and when a rocket range moved to the island in the 1950s the course was again awash with players, with army personnel and construction

workers making use of it. This continued throughout the 1970s, but as the 1980s dawned and the workers left the island, Askernish fell on hard times once more, only surviving the next two decades through the dedication of the locals, who maintained it for the love of the game.

Upon Gordon Irvine's arrival at Askernish, the chairman of the club, Ralph Thompson, proved beyond doubt that this was indeed a Tom Morris–designed course and, together with greenkeeper Colin Macgregor, they inspected the land where the original course was believed to have been. Irvine was taken aback by the beauty and quality of the land so much that he declared it 'the holy grail' and led the charge for the restoration project, formulating a plan of how to bring Askernish back to its former glory. A group of dedicated local volunteers banded together to raise the necessary funds, and the rejuvenated course was opened in 2008.

THE COURSE TODAY

As it stands now, the course amenities aren't flash, but they're sufficient. A small course café has just been taken over by a local woman and there are a few items for sale in case you've forgotten your gloves or need to buy a few spare balls. We're lucky we booked ahead, as they've only opened up the clubhouse long enough for us to get our hire clubs. It's a trusting community, and we're told to leave the clubs around the back of the building if no one is there when we're done.

Having not swung a club in six months I am a touch nervous on the 1st tee, but the beauty of Askernish is enough to calm even the most fair-weather golfer's nerves, and the first drive goes straight down the fairway.

From the clubhouse, the course snakes its way out to the west coast. The rough is thick, the greens are more than a little undulating and tricky pin positions mean the course never lets up. Some solid form early culminates in a surprise birdie on the par-4 4th hole. 'I've got you, Old Tom,' I think to myself. But things change by the 6th as we stand on the tee, high on the hill, only the white sandy beaches and Atlantic Ocean separating us from the North American mainland. A narrow fairway awaits, surrounded by thick rough littered with rabbit holes, not to mention the howling winds and endless ocean. Three sliced drives later and I am content to sit this hole out. Losing three balls never felt so good; the usual disdain for the game that settles over the weekend hacker in such circumstances has gone. After all, I am at Askernish, on the course with my wife and two good friends. We have travelled to the proverbial edge of the earth and we have the place to ourselves. A tired swing and three lost balls are not going to get me down.

I meet a similar fate off the 7th tee. But we won't go into that because the 8th brings about another birdie and suddenly my tiring legs and weak grip are a thing of the past. Then comes the 9th, and so the cycle continues. This is no modern course layout – as the 1891 design would suggest – and the 7 consecutive holes played along the coastline into prevailing winds are enough to test the resilience of any golfer. It is in the midst of this mid-round stretch that the intangible qualities of Askernish come to the fore. The greatest evidence of this is the fact my wife, Anne, has a smile on her face the entire time as she walks the fairways with us. Having never walked a course before, her only previous experience with the game was an ill-fated thirty minutes at a driving range care of a

bet I won a few years ago. Initially not keen on this out-of-the-way sojourn merely to watch us play, she was won over by Askernish.

As we close in on the final few holes, the breeze is at our backs: a welcome relief. From staring down the barrel of the endless coastline, we are now looking across the fields towards Beinn Mhor, the highest peak on South Uist. In the distance we spot a father and his sons playing the first few holes, the only other players on the course. We briefly chat to the only greenkeeper on duty and meet his dog, Paddy, who follows us around for a few holes. It is as if this is our backyard for the day and our parents have left us to our own devices. In the distance, an old man wanders the fairways collecting golf balls with boundless treasure no doubt awaiting him in the rough. And so we reach the 18th, a long par-4 back towards the unassuming clubhouse.

Overall, Askernish is not the beast you might think it is. Yes, it is windy and yes, the rough is thick and abundant, but there are not many bunkers and the course is not overly long. This is a gettable course and there are birdies to be had (did I mention my two earlier?) if you can drive it straight off the tee and hold your nerve. In our two-man battle, Will easily won the day – but I had my moments, and can you really compete with a guy who tours golf courses for a living? I think it's fairer to say that the four of us shared the spoils of a great adventure to the Outer Hebrides.

You can have your exclusive courses but give us an Askernish any day. Granted, an experience like this takes a little bit of effort and dedication, as this is not a Sunday drive away from your back door. But there are Askernishes all over the world, if you are enthusiastic enough to find them. This is no private club: there is no dress code, the green fees are relatively cheap (about GBP40, or GBP60 with club hire) and there is barely anyone on the course. This is uninhibited golf that allows you to soak in the magic of the great game, while not having to break stride from your holiday.

Halfway Home

International halfway huts worth visiting

Words by Mark Horyna

Illustration by Mike Cocking

'Sit, sit!' Mr Somboon ushers me into an unwelcoming but rather comfortable chair in the shade. The smiling young woman from behind the counter puts down two ice-cold beers on the small plastic table in front of us, nods charmingly and retreats to her station. Our caddies, protected from the tropical sun by extra-long-sleeved shirts and huge brimmed caps, all of them wearing gloves, quietly chat and laugh in the background.

While the friendly but serious Swedish couple we have been playing with are eager to get on, my Thai playing partner Mr Somboon – or Somboon, as I am asked to call him – says 'cheers', takes a huge gulp from his bottle of Singha and, leaning back, stretches his tanned legs. Wiping his face with a still surprisingly white handkerchief that has been in use from the first hole on, Somboon beams at me. 'A very good par of yours. That is a very difficult hole, very difficult indeed.'

I'm not sure. I feel a bit drugged. The humidity is high, the sun also. This is my first round in Thailand after landing only yesterday. With the jetlag and all, I'm a little off-colour. In fact I'm sweating profoundly, and the three beers Mr Somboon and I have had each haven't been too helpful. I'm not used to on-course drinking. Especially as breakfast today was merely a bacon roll snatched from the buffet at the hotel, hastily consumed in the back of a wailing tuktuk amidst the exhaust gas–infused Bangkok morning rush hour.

I glance around. The place looks familiar: the lush bushes in the background, the bar, the fan in the corner, the fridge displaying fresh fruit and small Thai food specialities. Even the table we're sitting at. I could swear that the young woman behind the bar looks familiar too. Have I been here before? Suddenly, I feel caught in

some weird hedonistic version of Nietzsche's *ewige wiederkehr* (eternal return), wherein I will be forced to play golf and come back to this bar again and again, forever. Lost in thought, I peer up at Mr Somboon. 'I have been here before!' I must sound like a lunatic because, standing up, he laughs and answers, 'Of course you have! This is the halfway house!' The Swedes look startled, maybe even a bit scared by our strange interaction. 'Come, young friend!' the only slightly older Mr Somboon booms down at me. 'Golf is not only beer and refreshments!'

Historically closely connected to the classic out-and-in design of traditional links courses, the halfway house or halfway hut is an archetypal British golfing institution. While American readers might be more accustomed with the term being used for a sober house where recovering drug addicts and alcoholics might find refuge, readers from Britain and its colonies will have completely different associations. The expression halfway house will bring to mind the smell of bacon rolls and coffee, the taste of tea, buns and crisps. Depending on where you are, the quality of your performance and the importance of the match, it might even evoke the taste of beer and Wolfschmidt Kummel liqueur.

In the very early beginnings of our game, course routing would lead players out into the links and then – not always after 9 holes, but sometimes after only 6 or even 12 – would have them turn around and play the same holes back in the opposite direction. Only much later, when the game grew more popular and the courses more crowded, was the idea of split fairways introduced. The Old Course in St Andrews, for example, still bears witness to these principles. Even today, most holes, with the exception of the 1st, 17th, 18th and the 9th – aptly named End – play towards huge shared greens, some of them so large you hardly even notice the second flag. It was thus only natural that, after playing out into the dunes for a couple of miles, players would appreciate a place of protection against the wind and rain, to have a drink and maybe go to the loo.

All over the British Isles, halfway houses have been serving golfers for decades, some far longer. Many have their own specialities. Others are famous for those behind the counter.

Luxurious course Kingsbarns has a rather small but equally pretty little hut, whereas the halfway house at Turnberry's Ailsa course occupies the iconic lighthouse building and has been lavishly refurbished to match its new owner's idea of style. Mrs Forman's, one of golf's most iconic halfway houses, was sadly closed in 2015 after nearly 200 years of service and has since been converted into residential accommodation. Not exactly a real halfway house, but rather a pub next to the 4th hole of the Old course in Musselburgh, Mrs Forman's was one of the oldest golf pubs in the world and famous for its Welsh rarebit and rich history. Here, the likes of Old Tom Morris and Willie Park Sr would take their drinks and eat their post-round dinners. During a round, orders could be placed at a window near the green.

There are many places so steeped with halfway-house traditions and stories that visiting them just to have a cup or glass of the local speciality would justify the trip.

Heather-clad legendary English club Sunningdale, for example, with its Willie Park Jr–designed Old course and Henry Colt New course, is said to have one of the oldest existing halfway houses of the British Isles. Here, where both courses meet at their 10th greens, you can enjoy Sunningdale's famous pork sausages and also get your dog a treat. The club in Berkshire is not only well known for the quality of their two classic designs ('Happy indeed is the club that has two such courses,' as Bernard Darwin once put it), but also for its canine-friendly policy.

While Sunningdale's hut has been in use for ages, the St Andrews Links Trust has a modern food and drinks van positioned behind the 9th green of the Old Course. During one of my last rounds there, I found the coffee to be especially becoming – although my enjoyment of that thin brew might have had something to do with the blisteringly cold temperatures that morning. The van at the end of the loop also conveniently caters for the New Course, whose 6th and 7th holes run nearby. It might sound strange, but the mobile hut is part of a deep-seated tradition.

In the late 19th century, an elderly gentleman named 'Old Da' Anderson, a former St Andrews keeper of the green, would take a barrow to sell food, drinks and golf balls out to the Old Course's 4th hole. And although local folklore will tell you that he also had much stronger stuff on offer, the hole has since been called Ginger Beer.

Up north from St Andrews is another must-visit halfway house. Still rather new, the hut at Royal Dornoch has come to some fame (people have even got married there). Nestled against the dunes between the 9th and 10th hole of the classic links Championship course, this modern affair, built to meet strict environmental regulations, can easily be missed – especially if you are brooding over your bad score on the tough first 9. But give yourself a few minutes to relax and take in the stunning views over the Dornoch Firth. They're well worth it. Besides, there is more trouble and sorrow ahead on the tricky little 10th hole, a 146 yard downhill par-3 named Fuaran. Those playing behind you will closely observe your ordeals whilst sipping their drinks and chewing their Mars bars by the hut – it might just be a good idea to grab a beer for later.

In America, where consuming alcohol while playing golf is more commonly practised and so-called beer-cart girls can be found scooting around many courses, the halfway house (or snack shack) has widely evolved from a shed-like structure to a sometimes fully grown building resembling a bar, with comfortable indoor seating and fully functional kitchens. Depending on which part of the US you are in, you'll find a wide array of local specialities on offer: the halfway house at legendary Pine Valley, New Jersey, for example, serves a signature dish of snapper soup. Surprisingly the eponymous snapper is not fish, but turtle. Topped off with a splash of sherry, the soup has been called one of the best halfway choices in the States.

Other clubs offer hot dogs, spicy chicken wings, burgers, burritos and sandwiches. And, of course, beer, lots of beer, most of it dubbed light but tasting peculiarly like full strength.

In Germany, where I've been living and playing for the last couple of years, golf and booze are well loved but barely ever mixed – at least not on course. Naturally, Germany has virtually no seaside links layouts and the majority of the tracks have loop routings that will bring you back to the clubhouse after 9 holes. Although halfway houses are not completely unheard of here, they are an oddity: something you will most probably find at clubs with 27 or more holes. After 9 holes, you'll usually have a chance to grab a quick takeaway coffee from the clubhouse, but you won't find many players taking a longer break – and you will most likely be looked down upon if you do.

In Spain, on the other hand, where the double-loop design is also quite common, you might find one of the following: food carts and telephones. Far from the clichéd, flimsily dressed cart girls depicted in Hollywood movies and in embarrassingly raunchy jokes told by elderly American golf acquaintances we'd rather not be seen with, these fine ladies (and the occasional gent) will offer savoury bocadillos with Serrano ham and Manchego cheese. Then they'll entice you with beer, soft drinks and sometimes even an expertly brewed fresh cortado from the on-board coffee machine.

The aforementioned telephone is something we first came across on Mallorca in the Balearic Islands. On the 9th hole of Son Gual, for example (a fairly new and beautiful development only a few minutes from the island's busy airport), there's a pole with a phone box attached. From here, you can call the clubhouse's bistro and order from the menu. Before proceeding to the 10th hole, you pick up the order at the bar. It feels a little strange, but it does speed things up a bit.

Back in the hot Bangkok sun, Johann, the Swedish gentleman playing with us, is already on the next tee. Taking practice swings, he says his finely tuned sequence is somewhat out of sync. 'It's the waiting,' he tells us, 'always this waiting. It stresses me.' We gaze down the fairway to where a 5-ball of Korean gentlemen are leisurely approaching their second shots. Each man is accompanied by two caddies: one pushing the trolley, the second holding an umbrella.

It seems we've been on the course for ages. But time doesn't matter here. The wonderful people of Thailand have a few passions that express themselves perfectly in golf. Food is one of those passions; hospitality and service are others.

So while in the rest of the golfing world you will normally pass the halfway house maybe once during your round, many courses in Thailand are designed in smaller loops. The routing will nearly always bring you back to one of several refreshment houses. So even if you're feeling a little giddy or disoriented, don't worry. Chances are, you're not hallucinating or in a time loop, you are just experiencing halfway house deja vu – Thai style. ⛳

A Golfing Honeymoon

WEST COAST
· ·
IRELAND

For two newly wed golfers, it made perfect sense to spend their honeymoon playing golf and discovering the charm of the west coast of Ireland.

Photography by Christian Hafer

↑

*Golfers at Tralee Golf
Course.*

→

Tee signs at Portmarnock.

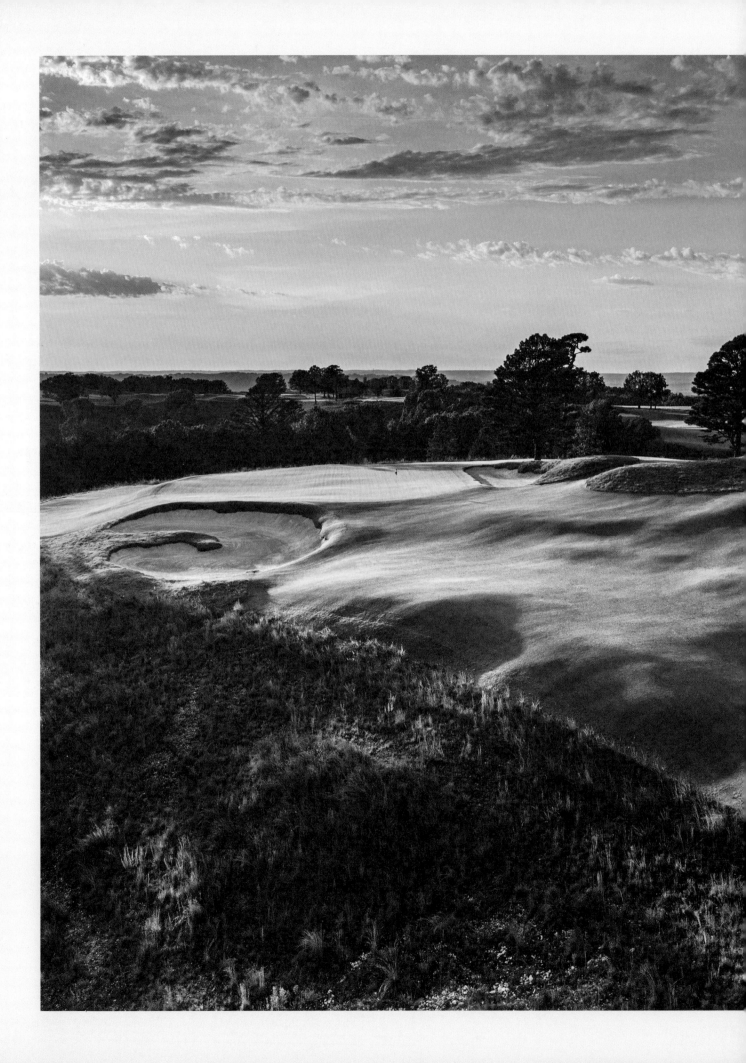

Big Cedar Lodge

MISSOURI

· ·

U.S.A.

There's a clash happening right now in the mountains above Missouri's famed Ozarks.

Words & Photography by William Watt

←

Extreme teeing grounds
at Payne's Valley.

Unlike some of the historical meetings on these lands, today's battle is not with guns and spears, but with golf philosophies and bulldozers. Chiefs Bill Coore and Ben Crenshaw have put their stake in the ground with Ozarks National: a wonderfully flowing golf course that embraces the land and floats above misty valleys. Not far away, there's a cowboy at work on an entirely different philosophy: Tiger Woods and his latest creation at Payne's Valley, which is utterly spectacular at every turn, with a swagger and boldness that's guaranteed to raise eyebrows everywhere.

Could there be a greater contrast in style between two championship golf courses on the same property anywhere else in the world? Debates will rage among the destination-golf nerds (like us), who will flock here to play some of the most compelling golf in the world. It begs the question: what speaks to your soul more? The light touch, natural beauty and intangible feel of the Coore and Crenshaw design? Or Tiger's course, with all the bravado and style that won him so many tournaments as a player? Subtle or bold? Reserved or expansive? Traditional or contemporary?

As well as the self-made success story of the owner of the world's largest chains of outdoor equipment stores, you could say that Johnny Morris is the link between all the action up here at the Ozarks. As the aesthetic brain behind Big Cedar Lodge, the resort on the ground and in the middle of the Ozarks juggernaut, Morris's story is as diverse as it is interesting.

Starting out by selling fish bait from his father's liquor store, Morris went on to become the Henry Ford of recreational boating in the US. A committed conservationist, Morris is intently focused on creating a legacy in the land here in the Ozarks of Missouri, not far from that first fishing bait shop and his childhood home of Springfield. He has built one of the largest and most lovingly presented private collections of Native American artefacts that you'll find anywhere in the US. Plus, his fingerprints are everywhere at Big Cedar. He famously hand paints every wayfinding sign at the resort, from 'Please Slow Down' to 'Payne's Valley – Coming soon'.

Today, Morris's mission of bringing Americans into the great outdoors takes many forms. His chain of over 200 Bass Pro Shops and Cabela's around the US is a far cry from his humble beginnings – these stores are the definition of a shopping experience. The Springfield store is a sprawling series of halls filled with every type of outdoor equipment you could possibly imagine. There are literally thousands of fishing rods, lures and, yes, you can still get bait here too. Pride of place is the line of recreational boats designed for a day out on the lake fishing or socialising with friends. The boats are constructed in the US and remain the highest selling brand in their category. There's a camping store, a hiking zone, and an extravagant hunting hall, where you can pick up guns, crossbows and all the ammunition you might need to get really close to nature.

But in a time where the digital world is growing exponentially and people are dealing with ever increasing screen time, what Morris really wants you to realise is that nature is where true beauty lies. And he is relentless in spreading that message in any way that will appeal to your senses.

An example of Morris's philosophy in action is one of the offerings at Big Cedar's Top of the Rock restaurant and museum complex: a self-driven golf cart tour of some of the most interesting parts of the property. The Lost Canyon Cave and Nature Trail winds through a cave formation, under waterfalls and over huge ravines. That some of these waterfalls are pumped, and the cave formations have been enlarged to accommodate the cart path, might well put off a nature purist. But Morris has a different target market in mind. He knows not everyone will hike five miles to see a waterfall. But bring them to a beautiful resort and offer them a fun way to drive there and see it with their own eyes, maybe they'll become a nature lover. It's like a gateway drug to nature loving.

Echoes of this philosophy can be seen with his approach to golf. The 9-hole course at Top of the Rock weaves around the restaurant and museum and allows people who have never played golf to be as close to the action as possible. They become part of the round even while eating lunch, seeing tee shots just metres away, and often joining in with applause or occasionally good-natured booing.

The course at Top of the Rock is a condensed mini Augusta-like playground. It's what a course designed by Walt Disney might look like – the rolling cart paths take you through forests and gardens between holes, and are as much a part of the experience as the golf. The stunning vistas, waterfalls, rock formations, immaculate playing surfaces (and yes, an island green), are a distilled version of American golf, presented to the non-golfing public as if to fulfill their dreams of what golf is. Morris is saying: 'Look at how amazing this is; be a part of it.'

TOP OF THE MOUNTAIN TOP

The two 18-hole offerings (actually, Payne's Valley will be 19 holes, with a jaw-dropping cliffside par-3 to settle any bets on) are being added to an existing stable that comprises the 18-hole Buffalo Ridge (a Tom Fazio–Johnny Morris collaboration), a 13-hole Gary Player par-3 course called Mountain Top, and the aforementioned original Jack Nicklaus Signature 9-hole course at Top of the Rock. If variety is your thing, no other golf destination in the world offers the breadth of golf experiences like Big Cedar.

Let's take the two short courses, Top of the Rock and Mountain Top, as examples.

Top of the Rock is a cart-only, carefully curated 9-hole experience where golf is presented as almost a way to explore the stunning garden setting. There are secluded corners, tunnels of canopy, lush crosshatched fairways, flowerbeds, paved pathways and steps, and crushed marble bunkers. There's theatre, with the watching diners, and drama from the lake views and bold architecture.

By contrast, Mountain Top is a 13-hole walking-only par-3 course, as demanded by the evergreen Gary Player – it's no surprise that his idea of golf involves a fitness component. Meandering across the highest point of the property, this is a compact, fun and no-fuss course that makes the most of the views. It's a favourite of resort staff who consider it a hidden gem for its challenging greens and sunset views. Play both of these courses back to back, and you'll wonder if you're even playing the same game, let alone in the same country.

OZARKS NATIONAL

It says a lot about the reputation of Coore and Crenshaw that their commission at Big Cedar for Ozarks National has brought enough gravity to the golf offering here that it can no longer be dismissed as just resort golf. So selective about which projects to work on and whom they work with, Coore and Crenshaw have the ability to shine a light on a destination like only a handful of designers in the world today. If they can convince me to travel 15,000 kilometres to see it, it should garner a pretty good following from places much nearer.

←
The 'pearl necklace' bunkers on the par-4 15th at Ozarks National.

↗
Room details at Big Cedar Lodge, including a photo of Gary, Jack, Arnold and Tom.

After a short drive across from the Mountain Top clubhouse, the Ozarks National clubhouse comes into view: a beautifully restored log cabin–style building purchased by Morris from another state and transported to the site. It now sits on the land like it's always been here, a trend that's set to continue as the round unfolds. To walk or to ride a cart shouldn't be a question here – despite the rugged terrain, this is a truly walkable course with excellent green to tee connections on almost every hole. It's a shame to miss out on these moments by riding in a cart, but given the searing summer temperatures that can be experienced in the region, it's inevitable that a high percentage of golfers will choose to do so.

It's hard to wipe the smile off my face as I walk onto the opening tee – first out for the day, dead calm, a misty fog enveloping the valleys below, and pristine teeing grounds promising much of what's to come. The opening par-5 gives a good overview of what to expect here: a steep drop-off on one side, options for every shot, and perfect playing surfaces. It's a gentle opener – a mis-hit tee ball will still probably find the fairway, and a decent second will allow you to find the green for your third and 2-putt for par.

Turning 180 degrees for the par-3 2nd, we start to see the creativity and world-class greens shaping that we've come to expect from the team at Coore and Crenshaw, and finished at Big Cedar by long-time staffer Keith Rhebb. Keith was on site for around a year, and for him seeing the routing come together across the ridges and valleys was one of the unique aspects of this job.

'When Bill was first looking at the property, he already had the pick of all that land out there, but he asked Johnny if he was willing to purchase more land to really bring more of the ridges and valleys into play in a way that was still walkable. So they grabbed a couple of little pieces of property to finish off the routing. The area around the 1st green and the 2nd hole was one of those, and around the back of the property on 12 and 13 was another purchase. Seeing how that tied things together and allowed the golf course to flow as well as it does is pretty amazing.'

The 3rd hole takes us back past the clubhouse with a beautiful short par-4 to one of the most dynamic greens out there – tough to hit with drop-offs on all sides and a two-tier design. Hole 3 flows seamlessly into the 4th, a long dogleg right par-4 that reveals the first of several forced carries across the course into play. Unlike other ridgetop courses I've played, in almost every case at Ozarks National the forward tees will avoid the forced carry completely, and allow the higher handicapper to get away with an accidental ground game. But from the tips, there are definitely some challenging looks, and you'll want to have your driver dialled in before heading out there. A few times my tendency to try and lift a drive in the air over a deep valley surfaced, which of course achieved the exact opposite result (and an immediate reload).

The approach to hole 4 is where you can start to work a more deliberate ground game approach, with a generous funnel short of the green rewarding a more creative approach than simply hitting a number. It pays to start thinking about these approach areas as landing zones early on in the round. Like many of the great Golden Age courses, you are going to be punished here for anything long past the hole. Visually this is emphasised by nine of the greens being positioned with nothing but the valleys below behind – it takes courage (or stupidity) to take all the club you need when faced with that view.

The risk-reward drivable par-4 5th is followed by one of the most photogenic holes on the course: the par-3 6th, which takes a good 5- or 6-iron to reach, and draws your eye, and your ball, towards the trouble down the left. Hole 7 is probably the best par-5 on the property, although there are four strong candidates throughout the 18. The shape of the ridgeline here is just perfectly suited to the size and strategy of the hole, with the valley pinching in around 80 metres short of the green. It conjures up memories of some other great par-5s that *Caddie Magazine* covered, including Pirates Plank at Cape Kidnappers, or even another Coore and Crenshaw gem, the 7th at Streamsong Red.

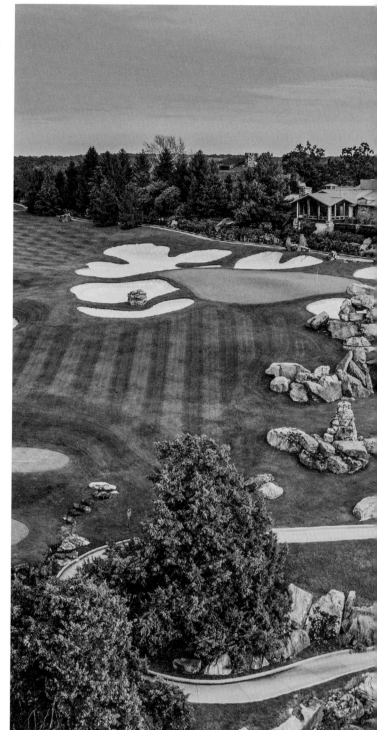

Another visually deluxe par-3 follows with the 8th, where a well-hit 8-iron will have you looking at birdie, which you might need – the par-5 9th is a brute. Constantly pulling you left as it bends left, the inside-corner bunkers and waste areas beyond are hard to avoid. This hole requires a stubborn stay-right strategy – as soon as you go left, you'll probably stay there, and have to battle it out all the way to the hole.

The 10th is a sneaky good par-4 that leads uphill to the third par-5 in 5 holes, and last for the day, with the testy 11th. Strategically placed pine trees provide a different look and challenge to this hole – attractive, but frustrating if a well-struck shot finds the timber. It's the start of the toughest stretch on the course. The long par-3 12th offers a massive 50 yard deep putting surface, but with most players taking a long iron or fairway wood to reach, every inch of it is needed. The forced carry on 13 is the longest and steepest on course, and links back to the main section of property via a massive wooden bridge that stretches across the ravine. A trio of intricate and strategic par-4s takes us to the show-stopping 17th, which has views for days across the Ozarks and plenty of hang time with just a wedge needed to reach. That view accompanies us up the 18th too, where a large ridgetop green offers a brilliant setting for the finishing hole.

There are so many terrific 3- or 4-hole stretches across the course that it's hard to choose a favourite section of the property, let alone a favourite hole. The variety, creativity and quality across all 18 holes leaves you wanting to turn around and head straight back out for another round. There's a feeling of weightlessness as you traverse the ridgetops, and the beauty of the Ozarks is maximised with carefully considered sightlines and approaches. At ground level there's a natural aesthetic that contrasts rustic prairie grasses with the pristine fairways and greens. Nothing feels out of place, yet there's a strong sense of place too. Coore and Crenshaw have embraced the Missouri mountains and uncovered 18 of the best.

↑

Top of the Rock at Big Cedar Lodge, designed by Jack Nicklaus.

PAYNE'S VALLEY

Payne's Valley is Tiger Woods and TGR Design's first public access course in the US, and the first in partnership with his long-time friend Johnny Morris. Aesthetically, it's clear from the opening tee that this has a distinctly different approach than Ozarks National: squared-off tee boxes, limestone rock features, and tightly mown fairways with multiple grass varieties. Tiger's involvement went granular here, specifying Meyer Zoysia for the main fairway areas, but with Zeon Zoysia used to provide a tighter lie for the approach areas. Unplayed at the time of my visit, but with the majority of the course already grown in, Payne's Valley looks stunning.

Standing on the first tee, all but the closing 3 holes can be seen as the course gradually eases its way downhill into the valley. Though it might exist, I can't think of another full-length course where you can see the next 15 holes! The routing ahead looks adventurous, bold and expansive. Tiger visited the site numerous times during discovery and construction and had a pivotal role in the routing and layout. This is a man who thinks big and, spurred on by Johnny Morris, for whom going big is never an issue, the result is a golfing goliath. Combining sharp edges and lush turf with exposed limestone, native grasses and, in the future, an extensive flowing river and waterfall system, this is golf on a spectacular scale.

But for all the visual differences, Payne's Valley actually shares the same playing philosophy of fun and accessible golf as its quieter sibling across the property. Wide landing areas off the tee abound – you can definitely let it rip out here, and it's clearly designed to be played firm and fast. Making the most of the natural contours and a more gentle overall gradient than Ozarks National, Payne's Valley might even play as the easier of the two courses once it's complete. Where Ozarks delicately traverses the ridgelines and valleys on its land, Payne's is more smoothed out. Yes, there are ridgetop holes here too, but the drop-offs are less severe, and the margin for error much greater.

By the end of the round, we're deep in the valley and surrounded by mountains and cliff faces. The imposing limestone cliffs that sit below the Mountain Top clubhouse form an incredibly dramatic backdrop to the approach shot into 18. This will be made even more dramatic by the release of a massive waterfall and the construction of the par-3 19th, which will traverse the limestone rock and leave no doubt that you've just played a life-changing golf course.

Flying home from Dallas, I'm reminded by tourist shop souvenirs that 'everything's bigger in Texas'. When it comes to golf at least, Big Cedar could be the exception to that rule.

↖

Gary Player's 13-hole Mountain Top course.

←

14th and 15th at Payne's Valley.

→

The closing hole at Top of the Rock.

→

(Next page) The two-tier 3rd green melts seamlessly into the 4th tee at Ozarks National.

Making Waves at The Cups

VICTORIA

·   ·

AUSTRALIA

←

The dramatic 3rd hole green site, which is becoming known as 'The Bathtub'.

→

(Next Page) The thundering surf of Gunnamatta Ocean Beach lies just on the other side of the dunes from the National Golf Club. Seen here during grow-in, the new course sits on the same land as the previous Ocean Course but bears little resemblance apart from the opening and closing holes.

Tom Doak returns to the Cups region thirty years after his first sighting to finally add his footprint in the area.

Words & Photography by William Watt

It's been over thirty years since Tom Doak first saw the dunes land between Victoria's Mornington Peninsula and Cape Schanck on Australia's Southern Coast. Known by Aussie locals as the Cups due to the unique humps and hollows of the sandy soil formations, it's an area that looks just perfect for golf. These days there is plenty of it, but that wasn't always the case.

As well as nearby St Andrews Beach, Doak and Mike Clayton first pitched a routing for the expansion of the National Golf Club in the mid-1990s. Overlooked in favour of eventual architects Greg Norman (Moonah course) and Peter Thomson (Ocean course), Doak would have to bide his time before jumping back on the dozer within earshot of the crashing waves of Gunnamatta Beach.

Today, the National is the Southern Hemisphere's largest private membership golf club – a behemoth that is likely to swallow one or more smaller Melbourne-based clubs in coming years. The membership, which forms part of the equity ownership model at the club, continues to grow in a market that has stalled or is in decline in many other locations. Such is the strength and appetite of the Nash that when the shortcomings of the Ocean course continued to become apparent – and it had been generally accepted to be the third of the three courses – it decided to act. Getting the large, heavily invested membership base on board with the change didn't prove to be a problem, with 89 per cent voting in favour of a re-design.

Tom Doak, now with twenty-three years more experience in the game and a collection of top-ranked courses around the world in his resumé, was brought back and given the freedom to explore the land as he had in the 90s. The result is a course that embraces the natural cups (or bowls) far more than the previous design, which instead had featured green sites atop dunes with drop-offs and false fronts hampering golfers, especially in strong winds. This is a design that embraces the fun golf philosophy of recent years, instilling confidence with wide fairways, and offering a helping hand every now and then with a generous contour or kind bounce back into play.

We caught up with Doak to discuss his return to the Cups region, what is in store for golfers at the National, and a few thoughts on his current workload and lifestyle.

When did you first see the site? What are your memories of this first sighting in terms of the potential of the land and terrain?
TD: Michael Clayton and I did a plan for 36 holes back around 1996, when the club was interviewing architects for the two new courses. I was always interested in it having seen that land beyond the original 11th hole on the Old course on my first trip to Australia in 1988. My first impression was the same as everyone who sees the Cups land – it looked like it was made for golf courses.

This first sighting was prior to any golf being built on the land – how did the presence of the Ocean course affect the routing you envisaged when commissioned for this job?
TD: It was easier to think of the raw land because I had seen it raw to begin with, and, since no trees have filled in between the holes, you could still see potential green sites pretty easily if you looked past the mowing lines that were there. In fact, on my third day of routing work, I stuck flag sticks in the ground at potential new green sites, and took the committee out and walked through the new routing so they could all visualise it on site, instead of on paper.

Did you consult your original plans for the course from your pitch in the 1990s? If so, were there any holes that were translated and still able to be constructed this time around?

TD: I looked back at the plan we'd done to see if there was anything we'd done the first time that we should use, after I had done my preliminary routing this time. But I found that Mike and I had only put 15 of our 36 holes where the Ocean course now is, and 21 holes where the Moonah course is – plus we had the practice range where the first fairway of the Ocean wound up. So it was impractical to use much of that routing for our new one – the start and finish wouldn't work. I did show Leigh Yanner my original 2nd hole one day – it was a downhill par-3 from the new 16th green to the 1st green, with the surf breaking behind.

Are there any other examples in your career of a course you have effectively designed twice in this way?

TD: My original routing for St Andrews Beach was a 27-hole routing for David Inglis; we wound up extending it to a 36-hole routing, though of course only 18 were ever built. Fifteen out of the 18 holes were on my original plan, before I first saw the site.

Were there any specific elements or holes of the Ocean course that you liked and used to your advantage?

TD: The starting and finishing holes made perfect sense, although the original 18th was very difficult and the members identified it as one of their least favourites. The big bunker on the old 4th was a cool feature, but it will be in play much more effectively on the second shot of the new par-5 hole. The alternate high side of the 13th fairway was something I'd seen twenty years ago, and I thought it provided a great option for the old 7th on the Ocean course, so you didn't have to hit down into the bowl with your second shot and then half blind back uphill with your third.

To what extent did you consider the relationship to the other quite contrasting courses on the same property? Do you feel it necessary to deliberately differentiate the style of the course, or are you more inclined to let the land dictate the style?

TD: I didn't spend a lot of time thinking about this. The bunkers and greens that we build, along with the routing, determine the feel of the course, and our style isn't that similar to the Norman or Jones courses next door, so I didn't spend as much time thinking about differentiation as I might if Bill Coore was building next door.

During the design and construction process, you put in a lot of work to present your ideas to the membership, including detailed maps and drawings posted around the clubhouse. How important is this in getting members to buy in to the project? Do you feel overly bound to these documents during the build process or more likely to follow your gut once out in the field?

TD: The GM Jon Gahan will tell you that it was a very significant part of the process. Honestly, it's one I hate, as I'm not a salesman by nature; I'm a builder, and I hate having restrictions on what I can build because I showed a different length on the scorecard that went with the plan. My solution was to put out the flags for my new routing and walk people around it. My office staff produced everything else ... but every page was full of caveats that we would make changes in the field during construction, and we certainly did. Those changes didn't have any real effect on the budget for the project, only the details.

What are a few standout holes on the new course?

TD: I think many people will single out hole 2, especially if they remember the same hole on the Ocean course – it's a much shorter par-4 and I think it's much more exciting than before, even though we kept much of the original bunkering and just moved the green site. After that, the routing skips over into what used to be the back 9, and it's harder for anyone to remember how the old holes compared to the new ones.

What are some upcoming projects that you are particularly excited about?

TD: At this point in my life, I don't really take on any project I'm not excited about. We are signed up to build projects in Ireland, New Zealand, Wisconsin and northern California. The first two are along the ocean, and the one in California might be the most dramatic land of the bunch. Plus the Sand Valley project in Wisconsin is a concept I've wanted to tackle for years – we're building a 6200 yard, par-68 course like all the ones I loved when I first went to England.

Alongside your design work, you are regularly researching, writing and publishing *The Confidential Guide* series as well as other books. How do you balance these pursuits?

TD: I love being in the field working on a new course, and I love to see new places for *The Confidential Guide*, so I've been trying to cut out most of my other business commitments – handing consulting work off to my associates, and saying no to promotional appearances, although there are still a number of those for the new projects we do. However, when I started up *The Confidential Guide* again, I did not think it would take so long, or that we'd get this busy with new projects again before it was finished.

My limit on being away from home has been 150 days per year, which has historically been the tipping point at which I'm exhausted at the end of the year. Ideally, I'd like to start winding that down to a hundred days each year in the future. All this travelling has been pretty hard on my body since it started involving longer international trips.

You used to be a reluctant traveller, however your Instagram bio says simply 'Golf Architect. World Traveler'. Can we assume you are now enjoying your travels more than ever?

TD: I was never a reluctant traveler, I'm just pulled in a hundred different directions and I have to say no to a lot of them. I don't want to be one of those architects that just shows up for a day and leaves all the real work to his associates; I really enjoy the on-site work, and that limits the number of projects I can do. I'd make way more money the other way, but it wouldn't be any fun.

We believe travel is an integral part of personal growth and gaining a broader understanding of the world. Have you found this to be true, and if so how has your extensive travel throughout your life opened up your mind?

TD: Until the last few years, most of my travel was in golfing countries, surrounded by golf people brought up in the same general colonial culture: America, UK/Ireland, Australia, New Zealand, South Africa. Plus, I'm an introvert, so even when I did travel abroad, it wasn't easy to get to know people. But going to places like Nepal and India and Kenya and Vietnam for the book [*The Confidential Guide*] has exposed me to many different cultures, and our common interest in golf has made it possible to get to know people in those places, which has been much more interesting, although discussing Donald Trump with civilised people is never much fun.

←
The 2nd green abuts the dunes of Mornington Peninsula National Park.

↗
Approach view of the 12th green.

→
The densely vegetated dune at the 8th green blocks any view of the green for those who stray left on their drive.

Languid in Langkawi

LANGKAWI

•   •

MALAYSIA

Just ten minutes through a winding rainforest road from the Datai Langkawi resort, we reach the Els Club Teluk Datai, the stand-out of three golf courses on Langkawi.

Words & Photography by William Watt

←

The Datai Langkawi resort is a rainforest retreat like no other.

Framed by the same rainforest system that envelops the resort, Teluk Datai (meaning 'Datai Bay' in Malay) is orientated in a V shape, pointing from the water's edge to the impressive Machinchang mountain range behind. Originally constructed in 1992, not long after the original Datai Langkawi resort, the course was re-worked by Ernie Els and his design team in 2013. Els opened up some of the sightlines, adjusted elements of the routing in parts and, somewhat controversially, removed all the bunkering, which was proving difficult to maintain during monsoon season. Echoes of the old bunkers can be seen on most holes, but in truth they are not missed. The short grass instead opens up the chance to bump and run if you find yourself out of position. The course also makes the most of a meandering natural creek system that runs throughout, which provides a greenside test on several holes, particularly on the back 9, and features regularly off the tee.

The ancient rainforest is a constant and welcome companion throughout the routing, providing a vibrant, flourishing backdrop, as are the birds and monkeys that regularly appear on the expansive playing surfaces. With 5 holes also making the most of the Andaman Sea waterfront section of the course, there is great variety on both the front and back 9 holes. The clever inside-to-out routing means oceanside and jungle-side holes feature on both sections, which isn't obvious looking at the course from the air. This means that the first few holes take up the most sedate land on the property, where a couple of fairly straightforward par-4s and a long par-3 let you ease into things. This is, after all, island life, and there's no need to exert yourself too much. The par-4 4th is where the course really starts to elevate itself from a typical resort course. Here the entire right side of the fairway is framed by the rainforest, the fairways feature surprisingly steep undulations, and a strategic green complex offers a glimpse of the ocean beyond.

It's on the 5th tee that we first bust out of the forest and into the steamy tropical sun, with the par-3 asking for a 6- or 7-iron straight at the ocean, and the Thai islands beyond. Out here on the double green, surrounded by tropical waters, and with two thirds of the round still to go, life on Langkawi is good. To follow, the back-to-back par-5s on the 7th and 8th are two of the strongest holes on the course. The 7th features a peninsular green site and requires a strategic lay-up to avoid a deep hollow left of the pin that would require a testing up and down. The 8th crosses the creek twice – first on the drive over to a flat fairway, then on the approach to a narrow green – again a strategic lay-up is required here. The creek also features along the inside of the dogleg-left fairway, making this one of the riskiest holes on the course to take an aggressive tack.

Whilst the seaside holes might draw most of the attention in photographs and tourist books, it's the inland holes, on the mountain side of the road that splits off the 10th through 13th from the rest of the course, that are truly unique. These holes do appear a little out and back, but given the tight confines of the walls of rainforest either side, combined with the more acute land movement on this side of the course, it's likely there weren't a lot of options for Els to mix up the angles. The 10th is the first of these mountain-side holes. Looking up at the clouds swirling around the nearby peaks and hearing the deep hum of activity of the rainforest, at times it's hard to concentrate on the hole at hand. Again it's a carryover the creek off the tee, before an uphill approach into a green that sits at the foot of the mountainous rainforest. The 11th heads back down the hill with an undulating par-4, before another impressive par-5 in the 12th perfectly frames the mountains and forces some fun shot shapes. The drive on 13 is also a delight, with a huge bank on the right encouraging you to let it rip and try to hit the speed slot, which can bring a short iron into play to hit a generous green.

Back over the road, the 14th through 16th are some of the tightest holes on course, with ancient trees framing every shot, and accuracy becoming critical. The dogleg-right 16th is a great example of this, with the forest pinching in around driver length and a beachside green making approach distances deceptive. The 17th is one of those truly memorable holes, playing a short iron over a small sandy beach to a green where anything right is in the ocean (the prevailing breeze off the water might help you out a little). Then the par-5 18th, back inland, sees the final appearance of the creek, forcing a little extra out of your second shot, and potentially causing some havoc in any matches that have come down to the last.

As we putt out on 18 a private helicopter lands on the practice fairway and drops off some guests for a hit, a reminder that this is one of Asia's most desirable islands. But Teluk Datai is refreshingly welcoming and doesn't present as being luxury. Much like the nearby Datai resort, the enjoyment here comes from letting the setting speak for itself, and just getting out of the way. The lack of bunkers is an example of this – with surroundings like these, it would almost be impolite to compete for your attention with bold features and hazards. Instead the course allows you to soak in every backdrop, every moment of interaction with the natural environment, and every well-struck shot. The Els Club Teluk Datai is a reflection of, and an ode to, the beauty of Langkawi and the rainforest that it calls home.

↓

The banded kingfisher (male, top; female, bottom) and great hornbill are rainforest regulars.

Golf on
Island Time

PLANTATION ISLAND

FIJI

This rough and ready 9-hole track on a tiny Fijian island might not be golf at its most glamorous. Still, bordering tropical waters and carved out of a coconut tree plantation, it's certainly not without its charm.

Photography by William Watt

Acknowledgements

To the *Caddie Magazine* founding team –
Dave Carswell, Jane Knight and Cam Hassard. This
book would not exist without your skill, passion and
guidance. Thank you for making *Caddie* something to
be proud of, and for the many laughs along the way.

To our contributors – thank you for your talent, your
stories, your ideas and your passion for golf and travel.
The numerous quality humans I have met and golfed
with through this project have strengthened my
opinion that golf really is the greatest game.

To our readers – thank you for supporting the little
guy, for recognising there's more to the game, and for
keeping us afloat.

To my friends and family – thank you for always
asking, always buying a copy, and for recognising
the effort.

To Pam and Joanna at Hardie Grant, and Murray
Batten – thank you for keeping our vibe, for making
sense of the *Caddie* madness, and for being terrific to
work with.

To Rosie – thank you for smoothing out the ups and
downs of the entire *Caddie* project, it's been quite a
ride. There's plenty more for us to explore and no one
I would rather experience it with.

About the author

William Watt is a freelance photographer, writer and
director based in Melbourne, Australia. Having worked
for extended periods of time in the UK, Europe, North
and South America, and Asia, as well as on multiple
around-the-world adventures, he draws on a wealth
of international experience and a lifelong passion for
photography in producing considered projects.

In 2016 William co-founded *Caddie Magazine*, combining his photography and design skills with a strong
passion for the game of golf into a twice yearly printed
publication. William is also a certified RPA (drone)
controller and operator, which has allowed him to
bring his creative eye to the skies.

Published in 2020 by Hardie Grant Books, an imprint of Hardie Grant Publishing

Hardie Grant Books (Melbourne)
Building 1, 658 Church Street
Richmond, Victoria 3121

Hardie Grant Books (London)
5th & 6th Floors
52–54 Southwark Street
London SE1 1UN

hardiegrantbooks.com

A catalogue record for this
book is available from the
National Library of Australia

Lofted
ISBN 978 1 74379 619 1

10 9 8 7 6 5 4 3 2 1

Publishing Director: Pam Brewster
Managing Editor: Marg Bowman
Project Editor: Joanna Wong
Design Manager: Jessica Lowe
Designer: Murray Batten
Production Manager: Todd Rechner
Production Coordinator: Mietta Yans

Colour reproduction by Splitting Image Colour Studio
Printed in China by Leo Paper Products LTD.